PUBLIC SECTOR
MANAGEMENT

PUBLIC SECTOR MANAGEMENT

Second Edition

NORMAN FLYNN

HARVESTER
WHEATSHEAF

New York   London   Toronto   Sydney   Tokyo   Singapore

First published 1993 by
Harvester Wheatsheaf
Campus 400, Maylands Avenue
Hemel Hempstead
Hertfordshire, HP2 7EZ
A division of
Simon & Schuster International Group

Typeset in 10/12 pt Ehrhardt
by Columns Design & Production Services Ltd, Reading

Printed and bound in Great Britain by
Biddles Ltd, Guildford and King's Lynn

British Library Cataloguing in Publication Data

A catalogue record for this book is available from the British Library

ISBN 0–7450–1263–9 (pbk)

---

4   5   97   96   95

CONTENTS

PART TWO

ACKNOWLEDGEMENTS

This book is a product of teaching and researching; it therefore owes a great deal to colleagues, students and the subjects of research projects. In particular I am grateful to Rik Common and Dominic Hurley, who helped with the research, Andrew Likierman, Stephanie Macauley, Liz Mellon, Ellie Scrivens, Kieron Walsh and John Stewart. I also had a great deal of help with the manuscript from Michael Connolly, Ashley Dowlen, Michael Flynn, Nicky James, Clive Miller, Alice Perkins and Andrew Puddephatt. I would also like to acknowledge the financial assistance of the Porter Foundation. Finally, thanks to Gus and F.-W. Fox.

INTRODUCTION

This is a book about managing public services in the United Kingdom. Why should public services be different from private services when what is public and what is private depends on where you happen to live? There are places where the fire service is funded through private insurance, and many others where it is funded publicly. The proportion of education carried out in private and public institutions varies throughout the world. What is provided free also varies, sometimes in surprising ways, in China, for example, fees are payable for education and healthcare.

In any case, what we mean by the public sector is not just a matter of who owns the means of providing the services and who employs the people. For example, half of road maintenance in the United Kingdom is carried out by private civil engineering contractors. In most countries more than half is done by contractors. But road maintenance is still a public service, in that decisions are taken according to criteria other than profitability and the work is funded through taxation. Defence is clearly public, but most of the bombs, tanks, guns and boats are made by private companies.

In this book we are mostly concerned with those services which are mainly or completely funded by taxation and which are not sold to customers at prices which produce profits. This is a very distinctive part of the economy because the 'normal' processes of producing goods and services do not apply. As well as public services not generally being run to make a profit, there is no competition in the sense of firms trying to entice customers away from their competitors.

Because these basic features of a market are absent, many of the principles of management which apply in the private sector are absent. Other principles, such as equitable treatment and allocation of resources according to need, pervade the processes of decision-making and management.

There is an accelerating process of reform of the institutions of the state in the United Kingdom, many of which aim to replicate some features of markets. Health authorities have been split up into service providers and service 'buyers' in the reforms now being carried out which has had the effect of creating relationships that are more like markets. Education authorities' powers have been reduced by the introduction of a national curriculum which controls the content of education. At the same time, schools are opting out of local authority control. Meanwhile, teachers' rights to negotiate their salaries has been removed. The public housing authorities are having their housing stock reduced through compulsory sales to tenants, and tenants are able to choose new landlords. In the civil service new arrangements have been introduced in which 'executive agencies' have been established which have contracts with government departments for service delivery. In any case, as a result of the privatisation programme, in which assets are sold to private investors, a large proportion of the public sector has been sold to private shareholders; indeed, in 1991–2 this raised £7.5 billion, or 3.5 per cent of total public spending.

For people who have made their careers in public service these changes appear bewildering and can be very discouraging, especially if they feel that the value placed on public service by the government has diminished. During the past decade public services have been described as 'non-productive' and a drain on the 'wealth-producing' parts of the economy. The result is a demoralised public service.

However, although successive governments have said that they wanted to cut public spending drastically they have not succeeded, and opinion polls have continued to show public support for most services. So far, the shake-up of public services has not added up to the thorough restructuring and shrinkage which politicians, especially of the far right, have called for. But the reforms and changes have raised serious questions about the way services are run and how users are treated. Managers and politicians at central and local levels have had to rethink the management of the public sector institutions. This book examines some of the new ideas about public services, to help people who work in them to do a good job.

Most of the reforms and changes have been based on two main ideas. The first is that public spending should be reduced, either absolutely or as a proportion of the national product. In Part One we see how far this has been achieved. The second is that markets are a good thing and that if a market style of relationship is possible, it should be introduced. In Part Two we see that it is never that simple. In markets there is a 'sale' which connects the organisation with its users. Businesses devise strategies and plans to ensure that sufficient sales occur to make profits. These plans are based on information about the buyers and what they can be persuaded to purchase. Success can be measured by various ratios which demonstrate whether sales and profits have been achieved. In almost all respects the public services are different. The task is rarely based on the need to attract customers. Prices are not normally set to maximise profits or market share. Investment decisions are not generally based on prospective profits. Motivations may even be different: managers and workers are not wholly motivated by earnings.

What all this means is that the values required to run the public services are often different from those required to run a successful business. For example, it is rarely appropriate to withdraw from parts of the 'market' because they are no longer profitable. 'Customers' who cannot afford to pay still have entitlements, which they would not have if they were receiving services from a business. Those entitlements derive from citizenship and social policy rather than from cash. Values of equity and justice have to play a part in management in a way that would be irrelevant to most businesses.

Part One is concerned with social policy and public expenditure. Chapter 1 is about the scale and scope of the public sector in the United Kingdom and the main influences on recent reforms, including the ideas of the 'new right' and of others who question the value of public services. In Chapter 2 we discover that, despite the commonly held view that attitudes to the welfare state and public services have become less supportive since the 1970s, there have not in fact been dramatic reductions in spending. On the contrary, since the Second World War a remarkably consistent proportion of national income has been spent on public services. The so-called 'breakdown in consensus' which is ascribed to the mid-1970s has not so far brought about large cuts in spending. However, the last decade has brought significant changes in social policy and some of these are examined in Chapter 3. Many of these changes have been designed to limit expenditure but there are other consistent patterns which emerge, including the introduction of competition, the promotion of self-reliance and the development of markets.

Part Two is about management in the environment created by these ideas and the reforms which have resulted from them. It argues that the public sector has to respond to the challenges described in Part One. Public services must be well managed if they are to retain popular support. Chapter 4 examines some of the markets which are being created and the strategies which managers can adopt within them. It shows that the real world is quite complicated, and simplistic notions of competing through price alone are seen to be inadequate. Managers need to develop approaches which are in many cases more complex than those of businesses.

Chapter 5 is about managing and measuring performance. Since public services are not businesses, financial performance is only part of the story, and efficiency, effectiveness, user satisfaction and other key measures need to be included. While some parts of the public sector have used performance measurement punitively, this chapter argues that performance management is a key management task which, if carried out positively, should have a major impact on the quality of services provided.

Chapter 6 looks at the impact of one particular sort of market reform, the introduction of competitive tendering for services. In it we see that competitive tendering is a great shock to the system and speeds up managerial changes. It also affects the wages and conditions of the people providing services.

Chapter 7 turns from the idea of competing for contracts to the question of how services can be made more responsive to their users. It shows that service design and delivery can respond to users even if they are not 'customers'. The emphasis in this chapter is on the importance of the details of service design, rather than the search for a 'culture' of good service. It argues that what service providers do is at least as important as their attitudes.

Chapter 8 addresses the question of organisational design and especially the issue of how decentralised organisations should be. It shows that there are no generally applicable answers, but that the appropriate degree of decentralisation is derived from the organisation's task and the environment in which it finds itself.

In Chapter 9 we turn to the future of the public sector and look at alternative scenarios which might arise from different values being dominant. If there has not been a breakdown in the consensus, there needs to be an agreement among service providers, users and taxpayers about what sorts of service they expect and how these should be provided. The chapter ends with a list of values on which such an agreement could be based.

PART ONE

1

PRESSURES ON THE PUBLIC SECTOR

SCALE AND SCOPE

The public sector is a very large part of the UK economy and employs about 5 million people. Table 1.1 shows where these people worked in 1991–2. Not all of them are in what we would normally define as public services, but even if we exclude the armed forces (300,000), the civil servants working in defence (140,000) and the nationalised industries, there are still about 4 million people. In central government, the major employers are Social Security, Employment, Inland Revenue and the Home Office, which account for around 250,000, or about half of the total civil service. Local government employs over 2 million people, including teachers. The National Health Service employs almost 1 million people.

If we exclude defence and support for nationalised industries, expenditure on public services in 1991–2 was about £212 billion, including the income support services of social security, which cost about £60 billion. Table 1.2 shows where this money was spent in 1991-2, and that the social security service is by far the biggest central government application of resources, followed by defence, then health.

The £52.3 billion spent by local authorities are predominantly spent on education, law and order and social security (housing benefit is administered by local authorities). Table 1.3 gives the breakdown of local government current expenditure in Great Britain for 1991–2. To put these figures into perspective, total public

3

Table 1.1 UK public sector employment, 1991–2, estimated out-turn (thousands, whole-time equivalents)

Defence	140
Social Security	79
Inland Revenue	67
Employment	53
Home Office	48
Lord Chancellor's and Law Officer's Department	26
Customs and Excise	27
Property Services Agency	16
Transport	12
Chancellor's other departments	12
Trade and Industry	11
Scotland	13
Ministry of Agriculture, Fisheries & Food	10
Department of the Environment	9
Foreign & Commonwealth Office: Diplomatic Wing	8
Trading Funds and Crown Estates	10
Population Censuses & Surveys	7
Education and Science	3
Wales	2
Others	1 or fewer
Civil Service Employment Total	**563**
National Health Service	970
Armed Forces	301
Northern Ireland	147
Other central government	56
Total Central Government	**c.2.1 million**
Local Authorities*	2,280
Nationalised Industries*	665
Other Public Corporations*	108
Total	**5,153**

*1990/1.
Source: HM Treasury, 'Public Expenditure Analyses to 1994–95: Statistical Supplement to the 1991 Autumn Statement', CM 1920, HMSO, January 1992.

spending equals about £70 per week for each person in the United Kingdom. Of this, £24 is spent on social security, £16 on education, £8.40 each on defence and health, £4.75 on law and order and fire protection, and £3.50 on rubbish collection and other environmental services. The remaining £5 is spent on the other items listed in Tables 1.2 and 1.3.

The finance for this spending is supplied in roughly the following proportions: taxes on income and profits and national insurance

Table 1.2 Expenditure by spending authority and department, 1991–2, estimated out-turn, £billion

Central Government Expenditure	156.7
Of which:	
Social Security	61.3
Health & OPCS	25.5
Defence	22.9
Northern Ireland	6.4
Scotland	6.0
Chancellor of the Exchequer's Department	4.8
Education and Science	4.5
Employment	3.2
DoE Housing	3.1
Foreign & Commonwealth Office	3.0
Transport	2.5
Wales	2.5
Ministry of Agriculture, Fisheries & Food	2.3
Home Office	2.2
Trade and Industry	1.3
European Communities	0.9
DoE other environmental services	0.9
Arts and Libraries	0.6
Energy	0.5
Other Departments	0.4
Lord Chancellor's & Law Officer's Departments	1.7
Local Authorities	53.3
Nationalised Industries External Finance	2.7
Total	212.7

Source: HM Treasury, 'Public Expenditure Analyses to 1994–95: Statistical Supplement to the 1991 Autumn Statement', CM 1920, HMSO, January 1992.

contributions and property taxes £28, taxes on expenditure £26, fees and charges for services about £6, the remainder being made up from other miscellaneous sources.[1] Of course, not every individual pays all taxes. Of a total population of approximately 57 million people, about 24 million pay income tax.

INFLUENCES ON THE PUBLIC SECTOR

The end of consensus

A conventional wisdom has developed that the various forms of welfare state in Europe after the Second World War were part of a

Table 1.3 Local authority current expenditure in Great Britain by function (% of 1991/2 estimated out-turn)

	%
Education	45.4
Law, order and protective services	14.4
Social Security	11.3
Other environmental services	9.8
Personal Social Services	10.5
Roads and Transport	5.6
Housing	0.7
Arts and Libraries	1.5
Industry, trade, energy and employment	0.6
Agriculture, Fisheries, Food and Forestry	0.2
Total current expenditure (£52.3 bn)	**100.0**

Source: HM Treasury, 'Public Expenditure Analyses to 1994–95: Statistical Supplement to the 1991 Autumn Statement', CM 1920, HMSO, January 1992.

'post-war settlement' between the trade unions and especially the returning soldiers, the employers and governments. In the United Kingdom a Labour government was elected, which was to look after the welfare interests of the workforce. Houses were to be built, full employment was to be established and maintained through macro-economic policy, a national health service was to be established guaranteeing access to medical care for everybody. At the same time there was to be a social security system which would look after the income needs of those who could not support themselves. In return, the trade unions were to make moderate wage demands and co-operate with changes in working practices.

Meanwhile, it was agreed that basic industries such as coal, steel and railways needed to be rebuilt and, because the state had organised production in wartime, this could be best achieved if these industries were owned by the state. Different patterns emerged in other European countries. In some cases, different industries were nationalised. Different institutions were used to provide housing, such as trade union or mutual societies. The role of state actions was the same, a post-war reconstruction by capital and labour in partnership, organised by government. This agreement, both on the reconstruction and the development of the welfare state, became known as the 'post-war consensus' which had the support of all political parties.

Then, the argument goes, the consensus crumbled because of the failure of economic policy to produce full employment and because the public services themselves lost the confidence of the public. Among others (such as Riddell, 1983; Keegan, 1984; Hoover and Plant, 1989), Nicholas Deakin (1987) argued that in the course of the 1970s the consensus on both economic and social policy was shattered by the introduction of Milton Friedman's ideas about economic policy and by the ideas of such bodies as the Institute of Economic Affairs on the role of the welfare state.

> The new approaches to economic policy which were developed in the course of the 1970s all involved radical changes of approach to the role of the state. . . . A recasting of the state's function was also a key factor in the alternative approaches to social policy which were being formulated at the same period, though with a greater degree of hesitancy. (Deakin, 1987, p. 73)

A publication by the Organisation for Economic Co-operation and Development (OECD) states that such an attitude is widespread throughout the OECD countries:

> These confident views about the beneficial role of growing public sector size and the efficacy of fiscal policy instruments in dealing with external shocks and market imbalances were increasingly challenged by the relatively poor performance of OECD economies during the past decade. Indeed, they have been questioned to the point where many now see the growth of the public sector as detracting from, rather than contributing to, over-all macro-economic balance and economic growth objectives. Scepticism regarding the wisdom of state interventions to fine-tune macro-economic performance now often coexists with a more profound suspicion that the growth of the public sector has undermined the foundations upon which the prosperity of market economies depends. Government involvement in almost every aspect of society is seen as jeopardising the basic behavioural norms and price signals which ensure the efficient functioning of the market. (OECD, 1985, p. 121)

Deakin goes on to argue that the disillusion with the welfare state extended to the civil service, a breakdown in the relationship between local and central government and a mistrust of the methods being used to manage the public sector. These are large claims. If they are correct, we should be able to detect major shifts in public policy, public expenditure and the role of the state after 1975, when the United Kingdom was 'rescued' from a sterling crisis by a loan from the International Monetary Fund (IMF), which had strings attached. The government had to promise to reduce the fiscal deficit (the gap between spending and tax revenues), hold down wage increases, especially in the public sector, and generally stop the expansion of public sector activity in the economy. These conditions are a consistent feature of IMF loans, whether to developed or less developed countries and whatever the relative size of the public sector. The usual result of IMF intervention is a major shift in policy. For example, in Bolivia there were large, real reductions in public spending, realignment of the currency and other dramatic measures, as a result of the need to negotiate a loan to cover a current account deficit. Among many other borrower countries, Kenya introduced a similar package. It is a standard cure for a variety of economic ailments and appears to reflect a worldwide shift in consensus. The OECD states that all the rich countries have a sceptical attitude to state involvement, while poor countries have the new consensus imposed on them as conditions by creditors.

The pressure from the IMF to reduce public spending occurred during the early stages of Mrs Thatcher's campaign to become leader of the Conservative Party. The reduction of spending and a general withdrawal of the state from many aspects of life became a part of the philosophy on which that campaign was based. Mrs Thatcher's supporters shared a set of ideas which set them apart from the old leadership, which had been involved in the all-party consensus on the role of the state and the activities of its institutions.

One of us?

After many years as Prime Minister, and even more as party leader, Margaret Thatcher still asks people the question, 'Are you one of us?', by which she means, 'Are you completely free of any doubts as to the utter rightness of everything we are doing?' (Pym, 1984, p. 19)

Francis Pym was one of the people who (with Margaret Thatcher) had been a member of Edward Heath's government, and joined the first Thatcher administration. He was dismissed in 1983 after the Falklands War. Writing a year after the 1983 general election, Pym lists the objectives which the government had set and failed to meet, including the facts that the money supply was out of control, public expenditure was increasing absolutely and as a percentage of GDP and that government borrowing had not reduced as much as planned. Inflation had been brought under control, but through a very severe recession and not to the same degree as had been achieved in other European countries. Public expenditure ambitions had largely been thwarted by the impact of recession on the numbers of unemployed; council house sales had been the one visible radical change in welfare state policies.

So what did the question 'Are you one of us?' really mean? It is important to establish whether there has been a consistent set of ideas to which ministers and party members could commit themselves. To find the underlying ideas we need to enter the world of political philosophy. That is not to say that government ministers rummage through the history of political thought to find a suitable set of ideas with which to rule; rather that convenient ideas gain currency at particular moments and are used as intellectual props for a set of actions. Sometimes the ideas and their origins are made explicit: when Keith Joseph was appointed Secretary of State for Industry he set a reading list of classical economics texts to his civil servants. On other occasions the implicit adherence to a set of ideas is enough: 'Are you one of us?' means 'Do you share our assumptions and beliefs?'

Ideas which questioned state intervention and reasserted the importance of market forces were clearly going to have a sympathetic hearing among politicians who were looking for reasons for curbing state expenditure and intervention. While there have always been economists and others who questioned the size of the public sector and the wisdom of welfare provision funded from taxation, these people were, until the mid-1970s, on the fringes of the debates. Institutions such as the Institute of Economic Affairs, a right-wing think tank, were outside the mainstream of policy-making and considered somewhat eccentric. By the end of the 1980s they were at the centre of government thinking.

Influential ideas

In 1973 Samuel Brittan published *Capitalism and the Permissive Society*. In this book he restated the case for markets as the best mechanisms for deciding what to produce and how to distribute products, and as ways of furthering learning and economic progress. In addition, he argued, the freedom of the individual could only be achieved through free markets. Individuals, reacting together through individual transactions, are the only elements in 'society'. Collective will or collective consumption are myths:

> The danger signal for the unwarranted extension of the political sphere is provided by the word 'society' in conjunction with 'modern society', 'society will not tolerate', 'social needs' and similar phrases and slogans. (p. 105 of the 1988 edition)

Since 'society' does not exist, there is no justification in principle for collectively provided services:

> There is no justification for the high moral tone sometimes adopted by those who wish education, medical care, insurance, and, in some cases, housing to be provided exclusively on a common basis by the state. What is there so elevated about a society in which take-home pay is for food and amusement only, and other essentials are provided communally on a free or subsidised basis, without the individual having taken any responsibility for them? (ibid., p. 128)

This book was an elegant defence of economic liberalism and summarised the case for individualism and markets. It acknowledged its debt to the trickle of writings by people such as Hayek, which had continued since the Second World War. The theme of individualism versus collectivism has been strongly taken up by Conservative ministers and Margaret Thatcher, who linked individual freedom with individual responsibility and denigrated state-provided services as 'the nanny state' which debilitates individuals.

A second important influence was *Britain's Economic Problem: Too few producers* by Robert Bacon and Walter Eltis, published in 1976 and, perhaps more importantly, serialised in the *Sunday Times*. The thesis of this book was that production of goods and services by the public sector was inferior to production of goods and services in the private sector for two reasons. First, there is no market mechanism in the public sector, which is therefore inherently less efficient in deciding what to produce. Second, since no profits were made in the public sector, there was no reinvestment to produce goods and

services for which t...
from the private to the ...
for goods and services a...
reduction in efficiency and ...

The argument continued tha...
booms faster as fewer resources w...
market, because they had been pre-e...
'unproductive' uses such as health and...
public sector had been expanded throug...
demand management in times of recession. ...
irreversible, as contraction of public services w...
facilities and making people redundant, which wer...
potentially unpopular. Hence controlling recessions ...
public expenditure led to an inexorable rise in the size of...
sector, which would eventually take over the whole econom...
book showed the rise in public spending (including social se...
and other payments) as a proportion of gross domestic prod...
(GDP) and introduced the idea that reducing public expenditure as a
proportion of GDP should be an economic and political target.[2]
These themes have been taken up consistently, although some of the
terminology has changed. For example, the private sector is no longer
referred to as the 'productive' sector, but the 'wealth-creating' sector.

As well as these two contributions there was a stream of less
elegant publications from the right-wing 'think tanks', especially from
the Institute of Economic Affairs and the Adam Smith Institute. In
books such as *Charge* (Seldon, 1977) and *Over-ruled on Welfare*
(Harris and Seldon, 1979), these members of the Institute of
Economic Affairs argued for a reassertion of markets in those areas
that had been taken over by the state. This was linked to the notion
of re-establishing the individual and the family as the centre of
responsibility, rather than 'society'. In the United States such ideas
were linked with the movement of Christian revivalism and the moral
majority who support self-reliance and the family against collectivism
and state provision, and support their case by biblical references (see
King, 1987). Such organisations, producing books and pamphlets
supporting the 'new right' cause are common in the United States
(e.g. The Heritage Foundation) and in Australia (e.g. the Institute of
Public Affairs, the Centre for Policy Studies), as well as in the United
Kingdom. Whereas they may not have popularised the ideas in the
sense of converting the general public, they have distilled a

and:

> For any particular programme, the more highly concentrated and
> visible the benefits to the groups concerned and the more hidden and
> dispersed the costs to the community as a whole, the better is the
> programme from the viewpoint of politicians and the groups with
> interests in it. (ibid., p. 50)

Since there is no such thing as society, any collective organisation can
only represent particular interest groups, and public expenditure
patterns will be determined by the relative strengths of those groups.
Individualism and markets for the production and distribution of
services would remove such distortions.

It is clear that such ideas have some influence on Conservative
politicians: a group of junior Conservative ministers and aspirants
meets regularly at the Institute of Economic Affairs in London.
Speeches about self-reliance and Victorian values of self-help and

family support are frequently made in support of actions to limit state involvement.

A fourth influence on government thinking was a growing concern about waste and inefficiency in the public sector. One example was the publication of a book called *Your Disobedient Servant* by Leslie Chapman (1978). In this book Chapman, a retired civil servant, documented examples of extravagance in the Property Services Agency in which he had worked and claimed that nobody, including government ministers, could do anything about it. Civil servants were too powerful and able to resist all pressures for change. This book generated a series of television and radio programmes during 1978 and became part of the discussion on the public sector in the lead in to the 1979 general election. The distrust of the civil service became part of Conservative policy towards the public sector.

Economic constraints

However, the task of cutting back the public sector was not to prove easy.

By far the largest single claim on transfer expenditure is the social security budget, accounting for about 40 per cent of central government spending. As an OECD (1985) study showed, the main reason for the growth in pensions and unemployment benefits was the growth in the number of claimants, not the level of individual benefits. Table 1.4 shows that the number of people receiving pensions grew from 7,189,000 in 1969 to 9,690,000 in 1986. The number of people receiving supplementary benefit grew from 2,690,000 in 1969 to 4,940,000 in 1986, while unemployment benefit was paid to 279,000 people in 1969 and to 923,000 in 1986. Given the level of unemployment and the age distribution of the population, a government wishing to reduce these elements of expenditure has few options. It can either reduce the entitlements to benefit or it can reduce the 'generosity'.

There was, however, a temporary respite from the combined pressures of a growing call on public expenditure and a desire to shrink the public sector and the tax burden. North Sea oil production produced revenues for the government which grew from £565 million in 1978–9 to £12,000 million in 1984–5, before beginning to decline. At its peak this revenue was almost sufficient to fund the whole of National Health Service (NHS) spending. The decline of revenues after 1984–5 led to renewed pressure to reduce expenditure.

Public Sector Management

Table 1.4 Recipients of social security benefits, 1969–86 (thousands)

Year	Family income supplement	Retirement pension (inc OPP)	Benefit Supplementary benefit	Unemployment benefit
1969	—	7,189	2,690	279
1970	—	7,525	2,740	302
1971	71	7,647	2,910	459
1972	82	7,793	2,910	352
1973	95	7,936	2,680	197
1974	70	8,072	2,680	257
1975	60	8,243	2,790	525
1976	77	8,417	2,940	587
1977	89	8,531	2,990	561
1978	81	8,667	2,930	492
1979	81	8,806	2,850	467
1980	97	8,970	3,120	940
1981	132	9,145	3,720	—
1982	166	9,232	4,267	975
1983	201	9,326	4,349	906
1984	203	9,362	4,610	896
1985	201	9,557	—	872
1986	202	9,690	4,940	923

Source: DHSS, *Social Security Statistics 1987*, London: HMSO.

APPLYING THE IDEAS

The 1979 government may have had radical intentions, but it found it difficult to bring about the changes which many ministers would have liked to see. Perhaps the 'public choice' theorists were right in one respect: it is very difficult to dismantle programmes which have well-identified beneficiaries and a well-organised set of people delivering them. Supporters of the welfare state included many members of the 1979 Cabinet and, to a lesser extent, the 1983 Cabinet.

However, reforms were made and we can identify at least four themes which indicate the influence of these 'new right' or 'new liberal' ideas. The first is that market mechanisms should be used wherever possible, even if there cannot be a fully free market for services. In many of the changes there are elements of the market mechanism at work, as opposed to planning, rationing and allocation. In housing there has been a move away from general subsidy and towards 'market' rents. In pensions the emphasis has been on individuals buying their own pensions, with the state scheme being a bare minimum. In education, the possibility of schools becoming independent from the plans of local education authorities is an example of a move away from planning and allocation and towards markets.

The second theme is that competition should be promoted between providers and consumers should be allowed more choice, including the choice to opt out of state provision. This would sharpen competition between the public providers and also between them and the private and voluntary sectors. Competition is seen as a spur to efficiency and customer orientation: monopolies can adopt a 'take it or leave it' attitude to their customers, whereas competitive businesses cannot. There has been a growth of private facilities in health, which has to some extent provided competition for the NHS, although there seems to be enough demand for services for this not to be a serious threat. The 1988 Housing Act puts local authority housing management into direct competition with alternative land-lords, tenants being allowed to choose their landlord. In the case of care of the elderly, private residential care was encouraged as an alternative to facilities provided by local authorities.

The third theme is the pursuit of individualism and individual choice, rather than collective decision-making. This principle is in line with Brittan's and others' denial of the existence of a collectivity in society. Hence, parents' choice of school, individual pension schemes and the individual's right to buy council houses, all remove decision-making from a collective level.

The fourth theme is that state provision should be kept to a minimum, while those who can afford to supplement state provison or opt out are encouraged to do so. According to this view, individuals should manage as far as possible without help from institutions of any sort, except their own families. Hence, increasing demand for services should not be matched by increased provision if this can be avoided.

In parallel with these policy changes has been an attempt to introduce a more 'managerial' approach to public administration. In the civil service there was a series of initiatives under the heading 'financial management initiative', or 'FMI'. These included trying to establish the costs of providing services and making managers accountable for those costs. Many of these ideas had been recommended eleven years earlier in the Fulton Report (Fulton,

1968), especially the notion of establishing accountable units of management. For some reason, enthusiasm for Fulton's recommendations was not translated into action. Various attempts were made to seek out waste and inefficiency to try to reduce costs.[3]

In local government the Audit Commission was established to oversee the audit of local authorities and to increase the amount of value-for-money work done by auditors. It also conducts special studies to find efficient ways of providing services. In the NHS a managerial approach was to be achieved through the establishment of a new managerial structure and new positions with the title 'general managers'.

The above elements have not yet resulted in a full-blooded 'new right' approach, with drastic reductions in the basic institutions. If there was an intellectual commitment to severely reducing the size of the state and its activities, and to individualism and markets, why has not more been achieved? After all, in other areas, such as the denationalisation programme, the government has successfully exploited its large parliamentary majority. The answer is that the process of reform meets resistance, both from providers and users of services. There were three phases of the government's action which were implemented at different speeds according to the strength of the resistance.

Phase 1: containing expenditure

The first phase consisted of attempts to contain expenditure: the early changes to social security were designed to bring some of the open-ended payments under control; the initial interventions in housing (by the last Labour government) were concerned to curtail capital programmes; changes in local authority spending controls, introduced from 1981, were attempts to contain aggregate local authority spending. The FMI initiative was mainly concerned with cost control. In these and other cases policy changes were based on the desire to cut spending, whatever other objectives there were.

Phase 2: weakening opposition

The second phase was to persuade both users and providers of services that change was both necessary and possible. In some cases this meant trying to weaken their support for the status quo. In the

NHS it still seems to be the case that professionals, especially doctors and nurses, are able to mobilise popular support against radical measures, in spite of the right-wing think tanks' radical proposals for restructuring.

However, attempts were made to weaken professional opposition to reforms. One method was to denigrate professionals. Failures in the education service were blamed on teachers and especially on their employment contracts. Ministers created the impression that teachers were feckless and lazy, in an attempt to reduce public esteem for the teaching profession. Similarly, civil servants were accused of not being sufficiently businesslike and of causing waste and inefficiency; important positions were filled by people from outside the service, thus blocking career paths and lowering morale. As for medicine, during the discussions of the general practitioners' contracts of service throughout 1989, doctors were also described as being lazy and interested only in money. The government increased that proportion of general practitioners' pay which is linked to the number of patients on their lists.

Meanwhile, relative pay in most areas of the public sector has been declining. In the United Kingdom and elsewhere there has been an erosion in the status and self-esteem of those who work in public services. Table 1.5 shows the relative erosion of public sector pay from 1971–2 to 1987–8, although the position of some public sector workers is much worse than others.

First, let us see what happened between 1971 and 1979. Public sector pay lagged behind seriously, with an annual average real increase of only 0.1 per cent as compared with 2.2 per cent for the economy as a whole. This means that if two workers earned £100 per week in 1971, by 1979 the public sector worker would get £101 in real terms, compared with the 'whole economy' rate of £119. Teachers, local authority white-collar workers and central government manual workers suffered a *reduction* in real pay.

If we look at the period 1979–87, public sector workers fared slightly better than during the previous period. Teachers, nurses and the police force actually did better than the whole economy. Civil servants, both manual and non-manual workers, fared much worse than the whole economy, as did local authority workers.

Taking the whole period 1971–87, with our two workers earning £100 in 1971, by 1987 the 'whole economy' worker earned £130, as against the public service worker's £107. The NHS ancillary worker

Table 1.5 Average annual percentage changes in real pay for individual public service groups in the 1970s and 1980s

	1971–2 to 1979–80	1979–80 to 1987–8	1971–2 to 1987–8
Teachers	−1.3	3.1	0.9
Nurses	2.1	2.9	2.5
LA manuals	0.1	1.4	0.8
Police	2.5	3.0	2.8
CG non-manuals	0.0	1.2	0.6
LA non-manuals	−2.5	1.1	−0.7
Armed forces	0.6	−0.4	0.1
CG manuals	−0.7	2.1	0.7
NHS ancillaries	0.2	−0.6	−0.2
(Weighted average)	0.1	1.8	0.5
(Whole economy)	2.2	2.6	1.9

Note: LA = local authority
CG = central government
NHS = National Health Service
Source: Bailey and Trinder (1989), p. 10.

would earn £97, the teacher £114, and the local government non-manual worker £90.

In the United Kingdom the civil service has found it increasingly difficult to recruit and retain the most able graduates as City salaries far outstrip civil service pay.[4] In London and the south-east of England especially, nursing recruitment is very difficult, partly because of the decline in numbers of people in the relevant age group and partly because of the relative pay for skilled nurses. Meanwhile, teachers know that the books and equipment they use are deteriorating and both they and parents are forced to engage in fund-raising to buy basic necessities. Numerous reports by Her Majesty's Inspectors of schools have pointed to the deleterious effects of low spending on equipment and materials on the standard of education. Health workers see that the resources of the NHS are stretched.

To achieve this erosion negotiating machinery had to be changed and, in the case of the teachers, abolished. Removal of negotiating rights is a rather blunt instrument but it does serve to change the balance of power between employers and employees.

A reduction in quality also erodes support for services. While this may not have been the intention of budget stringency, the result of underfunded schools and other services is that the public's satisfaction with them is reduced. There are probably limits to this process. Taylor-Gooby (1985, 1991) has shown that public opinion remains supportive both of public services and the idea of them. More specifically, the Conservative Party's supporters also favour and benefit from public services. Goodin and LeGrand's (1987) analysis of the changes in spending between 1979 and 1983 suggests that a Conservative government might be reluctant to impose radical change on those services used by its supporters:

> we can assert with a certain amount of confidence that the Conservative Government of 1979–83 favoured government services which were extensively used by the middle classes. This bias conflicted with, and in practice strongly attenuated, other policy goals. (Goodin and LeGrand, 1987, p. 166)

Griffith *et al.* (1987) believe that the NHS has had sufficient popular support to protect it: 'a daunting obstacle for right-wing populism . . . has been the high regard in which the NHS is held throughout British society' (p. 176). This was confirmed by the success of the campaign by the British Medical Association against the 1989 NHS Review. In July 1989, 75 per cent of the public were opposed to the reforms.

Phase 3: The 'new right' solution?

The third phase is the implementation of more elements of a thorough 'new right' package. This phase is referred to by Jessop as 'consolidated Thatcherism' (Jessop *et al.*, 1988, p. 19).

The first genuine 'third phase' occurred in the case of housing. The 1988 Housing Act effectively completed the reversal of post-war public housing policy, introducing market rents, choice of landlord for council tenants, and an end to general local authority new housing provision. While public investment in housing continues, it is at a very low level compared with previous periods and is primarily for people for whom owner occupation is not an option.

The reforms of the NHS also contain elements of a thorough market solution. Labour markets are freed from national bargaining as local agreements are struck. Competition is introduced between providers, both within the public sector and with private providers. The results of this competition became apparent during 1992, when some hospitals failed to attract enough 'business' to maintain their previous levels of activity and had to reduce their numbers of staff. The government held back from a thoroughly market solution to the problems of London teaching hospitals and set up an enquiry to decide which of the hospitals should close. Without the pressure on the hospitals to attract contracts and therefore cash, such an enquiry would have met the usual political resistance to change.

In Chapter 3 we examine whether there is a third phase in other areas of social policy, in the sense of a dramatic change in the services provided by the welfare state. Here we ask what a third phase, based on the 'new liberal' principles, would look like.

While there are various strands of thought in 'new right' writing, the populist form as espoused by President Reagan, Margaret Thatcher and European and other Conservatives has emphasised competition, market mechanisms, individualism and self-reliance, which imply that markets should be established wherever possible on both the demand and supply sides. The claimed advantage on the demand side is that people are able to maximise their individual welfare constrained only by their willingness and ability to pay, rather than by governmental budgetary constraint.[5]

On the supply side the advantages arise from competition for customers and profits. This competition allows enterprises to satisfy consumer demand efficiently, by looking for profitable opportunities and seeking innovation. Innovation may be directed towards inventing new goods and services or towards reducing costs.

The policy conclusions are as follows: there should be collective decisions about consumption only where individual purchases are impossible; there should be a large number of competing producers; and there should be free entry and (relatively) costless exit from markets by private suppliers wherever possible.

The choices of 'market' structure can be summarised in a three-dimensional matrix (see Figure 1.1). The options for supply-side market structure are that there could be a monopoly or many competitive producers, or some oligopoly position in between.[6] Demand-side market structure may be organised through individual purchases, private collective purchases (through insurance), or public collective purchases (through taxation). Supply-side ownership may be private, mixed, voluntary or public.

The 'new right' preference is for the supply-side structure to be competitive and privately owned and for the demand-side structure to

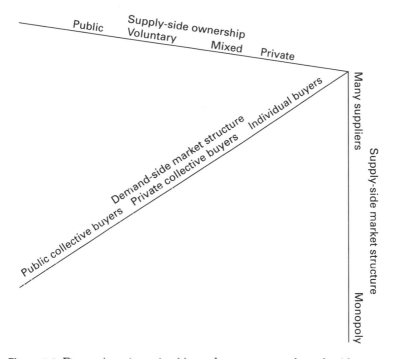

Figure 1.1 Demand- and supply-side market structure and supply-side ownership

consist of individual purchases. Where this combination is not possible, second-best alternatives on any dimension are acceptable, for example, private collective purchase through insurance from a voluntary sector supplier. Even if the short-run monopolies or near monopolies are inevitable, private ownership is preferred to public ownership. This consideration has been applied in the law and order services through proposals for privately built and operated prisons. Generally, though, the government is happy to leave police, the law and order aspects of child care, the probation service and prisons in the hands of publicly owned monopoly suppliers.

We have seen that the public sector has been under pressure from several sources. Many people believe that from the mid-1970s there was a dramatic change in attitude to the welfare state throughout the world, which ended a thirty-year period of growth and confidence. The growth in public spending was itself seen as damaging to economic growth and well-being, while advocates of individualism attacked the very idea of collective responsibility which is implied by a strong welfare state. These ideas were brought together by a series of 'new right' authors and organisations who advocated a return to a less interventionist state and to a society based on markets. Meanwhile, the civil service and other institutions were seen by many people as being inefficient and wasteful, partly because they were pursuing their own interests and not subject to adequate public accountability or control.

This combination of influences provided a powerful incentive for reforms in the public sector during the 1974–9 Labour government, and especially the Conservative governments since 1979 which presented themselves as a break from previous wet, consensual administrations. The Major administration showed every sign of being influenced by these ideas and many of their main proponents were appointed to the Cabinet.

We can now examine how far these influences have been effective. In the next chapter we look briefly at the approach to public expenditure of the last Labour government, which was in power when the 'breakdown of consensus' is supposed to have occurred. Then we look at the record of the Conservative governments to see whether they were successful in reducing spending, as they intended. In Chapter 3 we look in more detail at how they have followed their policy agenda, by curbing spending, introducing markets, increasing individual choice, pulling back the frontiers of state provision. In each area of social policy we see that radical changes were not possible immediately and that all governments went through phases of expenditure control and weakening of resistance before more radical measures were taken.

NOTES

1. For details of taxation revenues, see *Inland Revenue Statistics*, published annually.
2. This was a somewhat spurious exercise, since the transfer payments included in the public expenditure figure were not included in the denominator as part of GDP.
3. For more details of FMI, see Metcalfe and Richards (1990).
4. There have been parallels elsewhere. For example, Cumes (1988) argues

that through the 1950s and 1960s in Australia, the public service failed to attract the best talent.

5. In welfare economics it is assumed that individuals behave rationally and choose to spend their income on a set of goods and services which maximises their 'satisfaction' or welfare.

6. 'Oligopoly' is defined as the presence of a small enough number of suppliers for any individual supplier to be able to affect the market by its pricing or other decisions.

2

THE ATTEMPT TO REDUCE
EXPENDITURE

THE RESULT OF THE 'BREAKDOWN IN
CONSENSUS'

The breakdown in post-war consensus on social policy is dated to the mid-1970s. The OECD has shown that following the 1973 oil price rise, most countries experienced a growth in public spending (OECD, 1985) and, apart from exceptions such as Switzerland and Luxembourg, these increases in expenditure were not matched by increases in revenues and fiscal deficits occurred. It took most of these governments a long time to reduce their fiscal deficits. Some, such as the United Kingdom, achieved a fiscal surplus by the end of the 1980s while others, such as the United States, are still in deficit.

After 1975 there was apparently a major change in attitude towards the role of government. The Prime Minister, Mr James Callaghan, made speeches on a theme which has been taken up by subsequent prime ministers: state spending is not the solution to all economic and social problems and can obstruct economic progress. The first expenditure plans after the IMF visit were published in February 1976. These set out the government's intentions on spending up to 1979–80: a 4.25 per cent real-terms growth in total expenditure, but a 3.7 per cent cut in 'programmes'. The difference between the two targets was due to debt charges and increases in the contingency reserve.

Within these changes there was to be a 48 per cent increase in overseas aid and other overseas services (mainly EC contributions), a

24

5 per cent increase in social security, while most other programmes (except defence and housing) were to be cut, ranging from nearly 60 per cent in agriculture to 0.4 per cent in law and order. Table 2.1 sets out the planned changes between 1975–6 and 1979–80, along with those changes which were actually achieved. Overall, programmes stayed roughly steady, with social security, Northern Ireland and law and order exceeding the targets. Social security spending rose 17 per cent more than was expected because of unemployment and the commitment to give some financial support to the unemployed. Education and science was cut by 1.1 per cent over the four years, while health and personal social services spending was increased by 5.5 per cent. The major areas whose actual spending was at or below target were roads and transport, housing and trade, industry and employment. All these areas were relatively easy to cut

Table 2.1 Planned and actual changes in spending, 1975–6 to 1979–80 (1979–80 as % of 1975–6)

	Planned	Actual
Defence	100.6	98.6
Overseas aid and other overseas services	147.8	190.3
of which, Aid	—	113.6
EC contributions	—	5753.8
Agriculture, fisheries and forestry	42.6	41.3
Trade, industry and employment (inc. energy in 1979 80)	78.9	69.0
Nationalised industry capital spending	86.6	
Government lending to nationalised industries	—	131.0
Roads and transport	80.0	78.5
Housing	101.8	85.3
Other environmental services	89.3	88.4
Law, order and protective services	99.6	105.8
Education and science, arts and libraries	97.3	98.9
Health and personal social services	105.0	105.2
Social security	105.3	122.8
Other public services	99.6	94.1
Common services	103.2	98.8
Northern Ireland	95.2	107.0
Total programmes	96.3	100.8
Total public expenditure	104.2	103.2

Note: The plans at February 1976 were published at constant 1975 survey prices. The actual expenditures from the March 1980 expenditure plans were published in 1979 survey prices.
Source: This table is constructed from *Public Expenditure to 1979/80*, February 1976 (Cmnd 6393) and *The Government's Expenditure Plans*, March 1980 (Cmnd 7841), London: HMSO.

since they involved grants or capital expenditure. A large part of trade and industry spending consisted of grants to industry. Spending on houses and roads was largely capital spending. Stemming future flows of capital expenditure is easier than cutting services which are currently being provided. Cutting capital spending means not signing contracts, while cutting current spending involves shedding employees. If we look at what happened to the construction of public housing (in Table 2.2) we can see how easy it was to stop construction. There was a peak in dwellings completed in 1976, and then a sharp fall as reduced investment worked its way through to dwellings completed. The policy of reducing public sector house construction was continued after 1979. The reduction in completions per annum was 75 per cent between 1976 and 1983.

In cash terms (with no adjustment for inflation), current expenditure on housing went up between 1976 and 1979 from £1.55 billion to £2.5 billion (a rise of 61 per cent), while capital investment in housing by local authorities went from £2.2 billion to £1.8 billion (a fall of 22 per cent).

Apart from the reductions in capital expenditure, these changes do not seem to represent the watershed in the attitude to the public sector which has been proclaimed for the Callaghan government. The 3.7 per cent cut was not delivered and expenditure on programmes actually increased by 0.8 per cent.

A LONGER PERSPECTIVE

If we take a longer view and consider public spending as a proportion

Table 2.2 Permanent dwellings completed for local housing authorities, United Kingdom, 1970–83

1970	176,926	1977	143,250
1971	154,894	1978	112,340
1972	120,431	1979	88,485
1973	102,604	1980	87,968
1974	121,017	1981	68,139
1975	150,526	1982	39,879
1976	151,824	1983	38,830

Source: *Department of Environment, Housing and Construction Statistics*, 1986, Table 3.10, p. 49, London: HMSO.

of GDP since the end of the Second World War we can see that the mid-1970s were a temporary departure from the general trend. To make sense of the figures we need to distinguish between 'spending on goods and services' and 'transfers'. Spending on goods and services pays for such people as teachers, doctors, civil servants and the materials these need to provide services. 'Transfers' are expenditures which involve a payment from taxpayers to pensioners, social security beneficiaries, and so on.

There are different pressures on the two kinds of spending. Transfer payments vary according to how many people are entitled to pensions or social security payments. An increase in unemployment, for example, can result in an increase in spending. In the long term, spending on these things may be transferred to private pension schemes, but in the short term they are demand-led. Spending on goods and services is more discretionary. We might expect to see a growth in spending on goods and services during the period when the welfare state was being established under the old consensus. We would then expect to see a reduction when the consensus crumbled.

Figure 2.1 shows transfer payments and expenditure on goods and services as a proportion of GDP.[1] From 1947 to 1988, what we see is a remarkably consistent proportion. In 1947 the proportion of GDP spent by the government on goods and services was 19.1 per cent. In 1975 it reached a peak of 26.6 per cent (when GDP itself dipped in the post-oil crisis recession), but by 1988 it was back to the 1956 level of about 20 per cent. Figure 2.1 does not show a dramatic turnaround; rather, it shows a return to the trend from an abberation during 1974–6 which was caused, as in other countries, by the 1973 oil price rise and its aftermath. The annual fluctuations can be mainly attributed to changes in GDP, rather than to changes in the spending level.

'Transfers' are a slightly different matter. If we look at Figure 2.1 again we see that transfer payments varied from 11 per cent of GDP in 1954 to 19.1 per cent in 1968, then increased in 1982 to a peak of 23 per cent. There are three reasons for which these payments might grow. First, the numbers of people entitled to benefit could increase. Second, the proportion of those entitled who actually receive a benefit could increase. Or, third, the amount of benefit per person could increase. From 1960 the OECD (1985) analysed changes in public spending in OECD countries according to these categories. For UK pensions it found that between 1960 and 1970 34 per cent

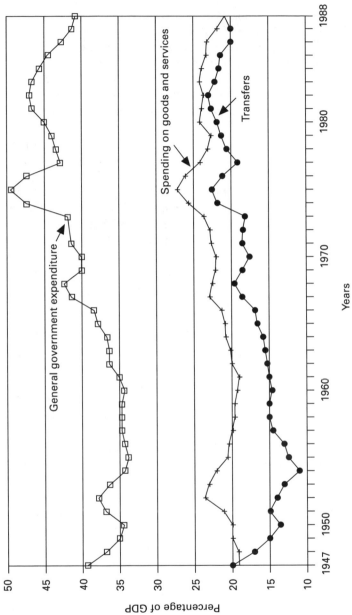

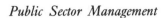

Figure 2.1 General government expenditure as a percentage of GDP, 1947–88

of the increase in spending was due to demographic factors (the number of potential pensioners), 40 per cent was due to the 'coverage ratio' (the proportion of the potential who actually received pensions) and 19 per cent of the increase was due to an increase in value of individual pensions. From 1970 to 1981 the corresponding figures were as follows: demographic change 40 per cent, coverage change 14 per cent and change in value of pensions 37 per cent. A similar analysis was performed in respect of change in unemployment benefit payments. Between 1960 and 1970 unemployment payments grew by 95 per cent. Of this growth, 68 per cent was attributed to an increase in the unemployment rate and 22 per cent to changes in the rate of benefit paid.

Between 1970 and 1981 the corresponding figures were as follows: expenditure increased by 192 per cent; the real level of benefits was reduced by 31 per cent while the unemployment rate went up by over 300 per cent. The United Kingdom experienced the second greatest (after Germany) reduction in the 'generosity' of unemployment benefits. During the 1970–81 period, when the United Kingdom cut its real level of unemployment benefit by 31 per cent, the average increase in the 'generosity' of unemployment benefit for the OECD countries was 12 per cent.

CHANGES IN SPENDING SINCE 1979

Apparently, the last Labour government did not produce the dramatic shift in public spending which might have been expected if there had been a real breakdown in consensus. We now ask whether such a shift was achieved by Conservative governments after 1979. One of the things which each government claimed it intended to do after 1979 was to reduce public expenditure. This intention had various definitions: it could mean reduction in real terms, after allowing for inflation, or reduction below preceding plans. The accepted long-term aim was to reduce the proportion of the gross domestic product (GDP) accounted for by public spending. There is a school of thought which says that the Thatcher governments were not as radical as their increasingly assertive rhetoric implied. At least until the 1987 election, people of various ideological persuasions were arguing that the Conservative governments had not made a radical break with the previous Labour administrations and that the

genuinely 'Thatcherite' intentions were blocked by circumstances and/or lack of the political will to adopt unpopular measures.
Peter Riddell thought that

> The Thatcher administration has never had a coherent strategy for shifting the frontiers of the public sector. Indeed, when Ministers were presented by the Think Tank with alternative ways of significantly reducing expenditure in September 1982 they recoiled in horror and had the paper withdrawn. (Riddell, 1983, p. 132)

Before the 1987 General Election Joe Rogaly argued that not much progress had yet been made in a radical direction:

> The Conservatives have tinkered with the Welfare State. They have not dared to abolish it. They have not even been able to reduce its cost. For in 1987 it remains more generous and far more expensive than anything the Labour government of 1945 envisaged – although much more tight-fisted than it was in 1979. . . . What they have not really attempted is truly radical change of the sort associated with the New Right. (Rogaly, 1987, p. 22)

From a different perspective, Joel Krieger argued that the Conservative government's policies on spending were merely a continuation of those of the last Labour administration:

> In aggregate terms, during the first 6 years Tory policy in government spending was not so much a reversal of Labour policy as a hardening of the inherited soft-core monetarism of the Healey/Callaghan years. (Krieger, 1986, p. 94)

Gretton, Harrison and Beeton (1987) analysed the size of the public sector assets and how the asset holdings had changed since 1979. They concluded that while the record of sales of nationalised industries has been impressive (realising £5.9 billion – at 1980 prices – between 1980 and 1987), there has been relatively little progress in asset reduction elsewhere:

> How far have the frontiers of the State in fact been rolled back? By international standards not far. Their major successes, achieved with

the nationalised industries, still left that part of the public sector larger than that of other industrialised countries. . . . As far as central Government, the NHS and local government are concerned, few activities have been transferred entirely to the private sector. And where the private sector has gained, as in education, at the expense of public provision, that has not always been the result of any specific Government policy designed to achieve that. Where, as in housing, the government could claim substantial success, the rump public sector remains much larger than the share transferred to owner-occupation. (p. 25)

Gretton *et al.*'s conclusion is that the government has been conservative, rather than radical.

Part of the evidence for the 'no change' school of thought was that public expenditure did not change significantly in volume terms (that is, after allowing for price changes) after the first Conservative administration. This was supposed to demonstrate a continuing commitment to the main programmes of spending. In real terms (adjusted for general inflation) spending increased after 1978–9. The overall position on aggregate spending and assets held is not necessarily the best indication of the government's achievements in containing expenditure. There was a deep recession from 1980 which put pressure on spending. Between 1979 and 1983, 1.7 million jobs were lost in manufacturing industries and there was a net loss of 247,000 jobs in service industries. There were also demographic changes, such as the number of people of pensionable age increasing by over 3 per cent between 1981 and 1987. These changes produced a large upsurge in the social security budget, which rose from £33.7 billion in 1978–9 to £38.6 billion in 1981–2. By 1991–2 social security spending had reached £54.7 billion and plans for 1994–5 were to spend just less than £67.1 billion (Autumn Statement 1992, HM Treasury, Table 2A.5).

There seems to be some strength in the 'no change' argument, since overall expenditure has remained roughly level since 1979 and changes have simply been responses to different demands. But the government was proud of the reduction in public expenditure as a proportion of GDP, from 46.25 per cent in 1984–5 to 41.5 per cent in 1987–8 (see Figure 2.2). However, this claim rests more on the recovery of GDP than on the reduction in spending. Figure 2.3 shows that there were small 'real-terms' cuts in 1985–6 and 1987–8, and in the plans for 1988–9, but the main cause of the proportionate

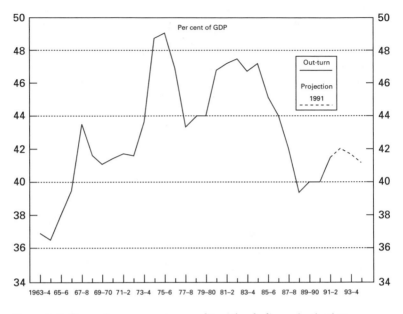

Figure 2.2 General government expenditure (excluding privatisation
            proceeds), 1963–4 to 1994–5 (*Source*: HM Treasury, 1992,
            Public Expenditure Analyses to 1994–95, Cm 1920)

cut was the increase in GDP. While there has been a successful
reduction in spending as a proportion of GDP, there have been only
two small cuts in spending in real terms in the years since 1979.

CONCLUSION

Since the mid-1970s there have been consistent efforts by both
Labour and Conservative governments to reduce public expenditure.
Both parties adopted policies which reflected the view that the state
should be less involved in many aspects of life. However, there were
certain pressures which prevented such policies from making a
noticeable impact on the overall volume of spending. The most
important of these were the rise in unemployment and the number of
elderly people who made claims on the social security system. In the
case of public services it proved difficult to make major cuts in
spending while maintaining service levels. One probable reason for

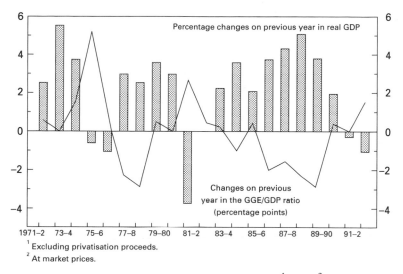

Figure 2.3 Changes in general government expenditure[1]/GDP[2] ratio and real GDP (*Source*: HM Treasury, *Autumn Statement 1991*, Cm 1729, chart 1.3, p.8)

this is that it is difficult to make significant productivity improvements in services such as education and healthcare which rely on people rather than machines. If a service requires a face-to-face contact, there are limits to the savings which can be made.

However, there were some fairly radical changes in spending and policy within programmes. While spending reductions were a major objective of public policy since 1979, the other elements of the Conservative campaign were also pursued. In the next chapter we examine the policy changes in the major areas of social policy.

NOTE

1. The actual figures for Figure 2.1 (% of GDP) are as follows:

Year	General government expenditure	Spending on goods and services only	Transfers
1947	38.8	19.1	19.7
1948	36.3	19.2	17.1
1949	34.8	20.0	14.8
1950	33.8	20.1	13.7
1951	36.1	21.2	14.9
1952	37.2	23.4	13.8
1953	35.9	23.0	12.9
1954	33.8	21.8	11.0
1955	33.0	20.5	12.5
1956	33.4	20.5	12.9
1957	34.3	20.2	14.1
1958	34.4	19.6	14.8
1959	34.5	19.7	14.8
1960	34.1	19.4	14.7
1961	35.1	19.0	15.3
1962	35.7	20.3	15.4
1963	35.6	20.3	15.3
1964	36.0	20.6	15.4
1965	36.6	20.6	16.0
1966	37.4	21.1	16.2
1967	40.9	22.6	18.3
1968	41.4	22.3	19.1
1969	40.0	21.6	18.4
1970	40.1	22.0	17.1
1971	40.5	22.2	18.3
1972	40.8	22.4	18.4
1973	41.1	23.0	18.1
1974	46.8	25.2	21.6
1975	48.8	26.6	22.2
1976	46.9	26.0	20.9
1977	42.5	23.6	18.9
1978	43.0	22.7	20.3
1979	43.3	22.3	21.0
1980	45.1	23.7	21.4
1981	46.0	23.6	22.4
1982	46.4	23.4	23.0
1983	45.9	23.9	22.0
1984	45.5	23.7	21.8
1985	44.5	22.9	21.6
1986	42.8	22.9	19.9
1987	41.5	21.5	20.0
1988	41.0	20.5	20.5

Sources: 1946–47: A T Peacock & J Wiseman 'The Growth of Public Expenditure in the United Kingdom' & C H Feinstein 'National Income, Expenditure & Output of the United Kingdom 1855–1965'; 1948–86: Central Statistical Office; 1987–88: Public Expenditure White Paper, 1986.

3

DEVELOPMENTS IN SOCIAL POLICY SINCE 1979

In this chapter we look at the main changes in policy, philosophy and service delivery in the welfare state under the Conservative governments since 1979. These changes have been seen by some to represent 'Thatcherism', a term used by both supporters and detractors of those governments to represent a particular combination of attitudes, including a belief in the family, self-reliance, 'market forces' and enterprise. Mrs Thatcher's more ardent supporters even spoke of a 'Thatcher revolution'.[1]

When John Major was elected as leader of the Conservative Party and became Prime Minister in December 1990 there was much speculation about whether 'Thatcherism' would be replaced by 'Majorism'. Would the new Prime Minister adopt a more conciliatory attitude towards local politicians, public sector professionals and other workers than Mrs Thatcher? In the event, there were no serious reversals of the previous administration's social policy or attitudes towards the public sector. Major presented an image of being very concerned about public services, and published The Citizen's Charter in November 1991, the period before the 1992 General Election (HMSO, 1991a). This White Paper had four main themes: quality, choice, standards and value. The mechanisms to achieve these improvements to public services were largely more of the same: privatisation, more competition, further contracting-out, more performance-related pay. Those mechanisms which were not a direct continuation of previous policy concerned the publication of targets and the degree to which they had been achieved, stronger inspectorates and better redress if services fail to meet standards. By the end of 1992 individual service Charters had been published for nineteen services, including the NHS (The Patient's Charter), schools (The Parent's Charter), the Post Office, the Employment service and Benefits Agency. The main emphasis of the Charter Initiative was on the idea of introducing competition or 'market testing'. All central government departments have been given targets of the proportion of their services which will be subject to competition with or at least checking against the private sector. In November 1991 another White Paper, 'Competing for Quality' (Cm 1730, HMSO) restated the emphasis on competition as an important managerial mechanism and set out proposals for the spread of competition to more areas of public sector activity.

When we look at social policy, we should remember that people, and especially politicians, do not always say what they mean or, indeed, mean what they say. A reform which saves money may be presented as a policy change to improve 'targeting' of benefits. Even if the underlying motivation for such a reform were to save money, politicians and their spokespeople would not necessarily stress this. The freezing of student grants and the introduction of loans were presented as a way of developing students' self-reliance and financial responsibilty rather than as a way of saving public expenditure. Similarly, managerial changes which are designed to achieve financial savings may be presented as ways of improving effectiveness.

Understanding recent developments is even more complicated when both the motives and the outcomes of policy and management changes are mixed. Better management of services may both save money and improve service to the users. Reductions in budgets can produce shocks which generate more effective use of resources, even while managers assert that they are currently performing at the best possible level. For those working in public services these mixtures are part of everyday life. For the whole of the past decade managers have been trying to provide good services even when budgets have either been reduced or have remained stable in the face of increasing demands. When budget increases were made, such as the very fast increase in the Manpower Services

Commission budget, or the growth in the Inner London Education Authority spending, these were either justified as necessary because of changing circumstances or condemned as profligacy.

This is all very confusing for the observer of these organisations who must look sceptically at stated objectives, which will almost always be underpinned by significant unstated objectives. For example, local authorities which have a long history of charging low rents for council housing believe in collective responsibility for the finance of public housing, but they also understand that tenants are likely to vote for the party which delivers low rents. Authorities which vigorously sold council houses may believe in owner occupation, while understanding that tenants who purchase are more likely to vote Conservative. We must also look for the actual consequences of changes rather than relying on what politicians or managers say they expect them to be. Who knows whether the policy of funding rents in private old people's homes out of the social security budget was intended as a way of developing a large private residential care sector for the elderly? For the users of the services such niceties are irrelevant: they are only interested in the results.

In each of the examples which follow we can see the four main elements of policy which we identified in Chapter 1: the desire to curtail spending; the belief in markets and competition; the pursuit of individual choice; and the development of self-reliance.

INCOME MAINTENANCE

The biggest single spending block is social security, which transfers over £60,000,000,000 each year. In 1989–90 almost 10 million people received a retirement pension, 12 million children received child benefit, 4 million people received income support and almost 4 million received housing benefit. The income maintenance system is clearly a huge enterprise, one which naturally comes under scrutiny when reductions in expenditure are being sought. It also represents the interface between the state and the poorest quarter of the population. While the Conservative government has not performed very radical surgery on the system, it has been estimated that the changes which it brought about within the social security budget between 1979 and 1986 reduced the potential expenditure on social security by £11.1 billion ('House of Commons library estimate', 1986, quoted in CPAG, 1988). While the main objective has been to control expenditure, reforms have also attempted to target benefits on those who need or deserve them most, to encourage self-reliance by reducing the scope of benefits and to encourage people to join the labour market rather than rely on benefits. There was also a desire to simplify the benefits system.

Spending control

When the Conservative government was elected in 1979 it inherited a review of the supplementary benefit system, which had been started by the preceding government in the aftermath of the financial problems of 1975–6. The review (called 'Social Assistance' and published by the DHSS in 1978) proposed to change the supplementary benefit scheme within existing budgets. No-cost reforms inevitably resulted in 'rough justice', by which it meant the entitlements may not always match needs, although this was also the case before the review.

Income maintenance policies have had several objectives but have been driven mainly by a desire to keep spending under control. In social security there is a potential tension between the idea of entitlements to benefits and the Treasury's desire to contain public expenditure. If the social security system is based on clearly defined entitlements and the service delivery system operates to deliver those benefits, the social security budget is very vulnerable to the changing numbers and circumstances of claimants. If the budget is set according to an expectation that not everybody will claim their entitlement, budgets can be exceeded.

This leads to a real dilemma for managers. If they produce an efficient and friendly service, they are likely to break their implied expenditure limits. Dual messages are inevitably transmitted to the staff. One message says that they should be 'user friendly' while they have to be aware of Treasury pressure to contain expenditure. While there is no formal constraint on the total amount paid out in benefits, there is an understanding that take-up is unlikely to be 100 per cent and that some claimants are more 'deserving' than others.

For a very small element of the income maintenance system the budget has been limited. The 1986 Social Security Act introduced the 'social fund', which replaced the old system of single payments for special needs. The social fund provides loans and grants for people in need, each local office being given a centrally determined budget or 'fund'. They must therefore prioritise the use of the fund, rather than use it for everybody who is entitled to it. This principle departs from the idea of entitlement according to a set of universally applied criteria: any claimant's probability of receiving assistance is dependent on the level of take-up by other people in the same area.

While the social fund accounts for only a small proportion of social security expenditure, it is worth examining because it implies a change in the principles and working practices of people in the income maintenance sector. The changes were introduced to limit spending. Tony Newton, Minister for Social Security, said:

> The Government believed that action was needed ... those considerations have been greatly strengthened by the continued escalation of single payments ... the most recent figures ... equivalent to an annual rate of ... at least £400 million. Many local authorities and other bodies are mounting campaigns to stimulate further claims. (Hansard, 21 July 1986)

The single payments to which he referred were for furniture, bedding, heating appliances and other necessities. They were available as a right to people who could prove a need. Local social security offices had the task of establishing need and authorising the payments. Since these payments were a right or entitlement, they were not in principle subject to cash limits. They were also an obvious target for welfare rights action by local authorities and others interested in the rights of citizens to claim benefits to which they are entitled. 'Mounting campaigns to stimulate further claims' might be seen as the job of the social security offices to ensure that people take up their entitlements. But this is not the case: such campaigns breach the other main principle, which is to keep the budget under control. The implications for managers and social security staff are profound.

Indeed, local social security offices were besieged prior to the introduction of the new scheme by take-up campaigns that were initiated by local authority social services departments. The resulting backlog led to single payments due to claimants being paid well after the establishment of the social fund system. The same was true of the 'additional requirements' system, which was abolished under the introduction of income support and replaced by client group premiums. These are flat-rate premiums added to the income support scale rates for those who are unavailable for work because of sickness. In fact, they ignore people with certain ailments and are sometimes paid to those with no special need.

The operation of the social fund is subject to the Social Fund Manual which sets down the rules of eligibility for the three main elements of the fund. The elements are budgeting loans, crisis loans and community care grants. Budgeting loans are available for claimants who have been in receipt of income support for six months and are to 'assist an eligible person to meet important intermittent expenses . . . for which it may be difficult to budget'. Crisis loans are to 'assist an eligible person to meet expenses in an emergency, or consequences of a disaster, provided that the provision of such assistance is the only means by which serious damage or serious risk to the health or safety of that person, or to a member of his family, may be prevented'. In both cases the loans are to be repaid out of the claimant's weekly benefit. The social fund was used to assist 1.5 million people in 1989–90.

Community care grants are available in a restricted range of circumstances for such things as repairs and maintenance costs, redecoration, furniture and other essentials to extend people's ability to stay in the community rather than being admitted to residential care. Local offices have a budget which consists of the estimated amounts to be paid, plus a standing balance for contingencies. That budget is cash-limited, which means that the local officers must have regard to the budget as well as to the needs of the claimants and the rules about priorities. Expenditure monitoring information will be used to 'judge whether it is possible to meet needs . . . of lower priority and remain within the budget, or if it is necessary to restrict payments to needs of highest priority' and 'SFOs [social fund officers] must always consider the state of the LO [local office] budget and should aim to meet the highest priority needs first. SFOs will sometimes be obliged to refuse applications in order to meet higher priorities within the budget.' To ensure that the inconsistency which this implies, especially during the last few months when the fund is running low, is not challenged, the guidance states: 'the flexibility of the social fund and the wide variety of individual circumstances covered mean that a decision in one case will not be a binding precedent for others.'

While the changes affect a very small part of the social security budget, they may provide clues about future directions for managers. The implications are serious. While clerical and counter staff are operating according to a set of rules, supervision is relatively straightforward. When a high degree of discretion is introduced, especially when the rules can change according to how much is left in the budget, the task of counter staff becomes more skilled and carries a heavier burden of responsibility. Supervision and control become more akin to that of professionals using a high degree of discretion than to supervision of clerical officers following a set of rules.

Targeting

The second objective is to make benefits more means-tested or 'targeted'. Targeted benefits remain the central element of social security. The targeting ensures that people who are not entitled to benefit do not receive it. Child benefit, a flat rate benefit for every child, was frozen between 1986 and April 1991. The rationale for the freeze was that not every child was in need of the benefit and the money saved would be better used if targeted on those in most need. It was increased from £7.25 to £8.25 per week in April 1991 and a further £1 was added in October 1991 because of pressure from parents and lobby groups.

There was little discussion of the take-up of discretionary benefits in the review. Family income support, which was replaced by the family credit scheme, achieved an estimated take-up of 50 per cent of those families who were entitled to it. In 1984 housing benefit achieved only a 77 per cent take-up.[2] In 1983 only 76 per cent of those eligible claimed supplementary benefit. If positive targeting were a priority, these take-up rates could presumably have been improved. But not if the attitude expressed by Tony Newton predominates, i.e. that people should not be encouraged to claim their full entitlement.

The idea of targeting is not just a question of ensuring that benefits are paid to those most in need. There is also a notion that some poor people are more deserving than others. Some people think that unemployed school leavers and single parents are a less deserving target than old people.

The framework of targets under which the Benefits Agency operates includes measures of the amount of over-payment of benefits but is less insistent on improving take-up rates and eliminating under-payment.

Self-reliance

In the longer run even old people, who are generally considered to be deserving, are expected to provide for their own incomes after retirement. The Social Security Act also changed the pension system, allowing (from 1999 retirements) people to opt out of the state earnings-related pension scheme, at their own risk, and take out a personal pension. These and other changes were designed to promote a free market in pensions. Already, in 1980, the annual increase in pensions had been decoupled from earnings and linked to changes in the retail price index. In the Conservative manifesto for the 1987 General Election the state pension was given a minimal, safety net role:

> retired people value their independence. They do not want to rely on the State alone for their income, nor, increasingly, are they doing so. We share Beveridge's original goal of a good basic pension from the State, together with a second income from occupational and personal pensions and savings. (Conservative Party, 1987, p. 52)

This third objective is based on the idea that state pensions and other benefits create dependency among the population. The state becomes a 'nanny' for those who otherwise would be able to provide for themselves.

The labour market

The fourth objective was to remove obstacles to the free operation of the labour market. If unemployed people are to have an incentive to take low-paid jobs, their incomes must be kept very low when they are out of work. As Peter Townsend (1987) said:

Since 1979 the whole development of policy appears to have been based on the government theory that the unemployed receive too much income and do not have sufficient incentive. The theory was never justified but it has been pursued vigorously.

The 1986 Social Security Act reduced the earnings-related element of unemployment benefit, stopped benefit for young people who decline places on training schemes and introduced an 'income support' system which takes account of personal savings and assets. Income support extends the social assistance principle which sought to 'make available the means of sustaining life at a chosen level of subsistence where all other means of doing so have failed'. The government had also introduced the 'Voluntary unemployment deduction' and had progressively extended the disqualification period for unemployment benefit. Furthermore, apart from withdrawing benefit to young people who refused places on training schemes, those in bed and breakfast accommodation were facing further problems. Already, those under the age of 25, with certain exceptions, were subject to locally defined time limits for which the Department of Social Security could pay their board and lodging, and even those payments were subject to, again, a locally defined upper limit; 1989 saw local authorities taking on the additional burden of bed and breakfast claimants, the Department of Social Security being only responsible for subsistence rates with the difference being made up from ratepayers' money.

Atkinson (1989) summarises the impact of the changes on unemployed people:

> Without public debate, there has been a shift in principle underlying income support for the unemployed. The role of insurance benefits has been eroded by the tightening of the contribution conditions, the extension of the disqualification period, the restriction of benefits to students, the abolition of the lower rate benefits, and the abatement for occupational pensioners; their value has been reduced by the taxation of benefits; and the abandonment of statutory indexation has made the position of recipients insecure.

Norman Fowler, Secretary of State at the (then) DHSS, described the reviews of the social security system, which led to the 1986 Social Security Act, as 'the most substantial examination of the social security system since the Beveridge Report 40 years ago'. There has certainly been a shift in the way in which social security is managed, although the overall level of spending has continued to grow. Income maintenance policy reflects all the elements of policy which we identified in Chapter 1. Those running the service have to respond to those policies. For example, the pursuit of self-reliance implies that the social security should encourage people to look after themselves. Meanwhile, the managerialist concern for financial control implies that managers should be increasingly concerned with budgets.

LOCAL GOVERNMENT

Central government has also tried to contain local authority spending and to influence its activities. Local government employs about 2 million people in the United Kingdom and is responsible for most education, personal social services, public housing, town planning, environmental health, trading standards, road construction and maintenance, libraries and arts. It accounts for about one quarter of public expenditure.[3]

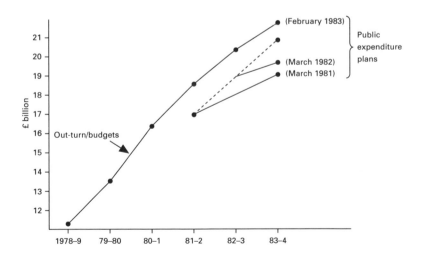

Figure 3.1 Local authority current expenditure in cash (*Source*: White Paper 'Rates', 1983)

Central control over local spending

Since 1975, central government has been trying to exercise more control over local authorities. The 1979 administration wanted to curtail the activities of local government further and especially to prevent any increase in expenditure. The Callaghan government had already imposed its cuts in capital expenditure, so the reductions had to take place in recurrent (or 'revenue') expenditure. The mechanism of central government grant to local authorities was revised many times, beginning in 1980. The problem for the government was that under the inherited rate support grant system,[4] if local authorities increased their expenditure their grant also increased: rate support grant was 'open-ended'. In 1980 the Department of Environment thought that if this open-endedness could be removed and authorities were to receive a smaller proportionate grant on additions to expenditure they could be persuaded to curtail their spending plans. The government wanted to ensure that local authorities conformed to the government's expenditure plans, rather than to their own. The public expenditure plans published in March 1981 set local government current spending at about £17 billion. In the event, local authorities spent about £18 billion. Successive plans revised the government's targets upwards, but local government overshot the targets by around £1 billion each year. The plans and outcomes are shown in Figure 3.1 The difference between the government's and local authorities' plans in 1983–4 was £771 million.

Local authorities avoided the controls in two main ways. They changed the way in which revenue expenditure was accounted for, thereby reducing the apparent spending on the revenue account through practices which became known as 'creative accounting'. For example, routine housing maintenance would normally be funded through the housing revenue account. This maintenance could be grouped together into large sums of money and reclassified as capital spending. Authorities also, especially in the early years, increased the level of the rates (the local property taxes) to compensate for the loss of government grant. The use of the grant to control expenditure was made more stringent, successive years bringing greater financial penalties for overspending the government's limits set for each authority. The impact of this was to curtail spending. As the regime became more stringent, increasing financial penalties were incurred for 'overspending'. In severe cases, an overspend of £1 incurred a loss of £5 of grant, a loss which had to be funded by ratepayers. Overspending the government limits became less and less attractive.

Since some authorities persisted in maintaining expenditure levels, the government then introduced (in 1984) a new provision. The level of rates itself was to be controlled in those authorities whose expenditure exceeded central government's idea of what it should be. Announcing the White Paper on the rates in August 1983, Patrick Jenkin, Secretary of State for the Environment, explained the government's view:

> I acknowledge the scope and importance of the services provided by local government. But local government's powers derive from Parliament. Local authorities form part of the wider community and should operate within national economic and social policies. Central Government cannot leave decisions about overall spending levels to local government. Neither can Central Government ignore the deep sense of grievance felt by many domestic and non-domestic ratepayers about excessive expenditure and rate levels. . . . Despite the pressures of the grant system local government as a whole has continued to overspend. We have therefore been forced to take direct action on the rates of the high spenders. (DOE Press Release, 1 August 1983)

This direct action (called 'rate-capping') removed the option of replacing lost grant through higher rates. It did not remove all the creative accounting measures, however, and ingenious schemes were devised in some authorities to reduce the apparent level of revenue expenditure. These included, for example, the sale and lease-back of assets such as parking meters and town halls in order to raise cash to cover shortfalls on the revenue account. In the end, most of these measures were destructive since they essentially involved borrowing for recurrent expenditure not covered by sustainable long-term sources of revenue, a problem which will eventually result from the central government's policy of funding current expenditure from asset sales.

Other authorities, especially but not exclusively those controlled by Conservatives, attempted to comply with the government's ideas on spending. The City of Birmingham under Labour and Conservative administrations has consistently spent less than the amount thought necessary by the government to provide a standard level of service. The rules for individual authorities changed with bewildering frequency, sometimes on more than one occasion during the financial year. The targets for an authority's spending and the consequences of exceeding the targets were changed according to the level of spending by authorities as a whole and according to the stringency of the rules.

Eventually the government honoured a long-standing personal commitment by the Prime Minister, Mrs Thatcher, to abolish the rating system and a new method of financing was introduced in the Local Government Act 1988. From April 1989 in Scotland and April 1990 in England and Wales the Community Charge (otherwise known as 'poll tax'), based on individuals rather than properties, replaced domestic rates and a national non-domestic rate replaced locally set rates on non-domestic property. Only the community charge and fees and charges for services, such as entrance fees for leisure centres, were now set by local authorities, the rest of their income being controlled by central government. Even the small amount of discretion initially allowed was soon removed when 'capping' was applied to prevent authorities from raising more Community Charge than the government thought appropriate. In May 1991, the government announced that all local authorities would be subject to 'charge-capping' from the financial year 1992–3. Fearing the reaction of the public to higher Community Charge bills the government allocated, in the March 1991 budget, an extra £4.5 billion to allow local authorities to reduce their Charge bills by £140 per payer.

These measures were insufficient to save the tax. The Community Charge quickly failed: it was expensive and difficult to collect and became very unpopular. It was estimated (Public Finance Foundation, 1991), that 11,600 extra staff had been hired at a cost of £232 million to collect the tax. There was a huge workload for the courts, which had to prosecute non-payers: 5 million liability orders were issued for non-payment in the first year. In Scotland 300 court officers had to deal with the cases of 1 million non-payers. It was estimated by the Office of Population Censuses and Surveys that 1.8 million people failed to register themselves at the 1991 Census of Population because they had not put themselves on the Community Charge register to avoid the tax and feared that Census registration would be linked to the Charge. It is most likely that they have all lost their right to vote for the same reason. There were large demonstrations against the tax, some of which turned into riots (see Burns (1992) for an account).

In April 1991 Michael Heseltine, then Secretary of State for the Environment, announced plans for a new local tax, to be called the Council Tax and introduced from April 1993. This is based on two aspects of a household: the number of adults and the value of the property. Properties are valued and put into bands, which then determine the level of tax. The collapse of property values caused some distress with this process since values were assessed at their 1990 levels before the big price slide had established itself. Rebates are available for people unable to pay. The tax is subject to capping by the government.

The effect of these taxation changes on local authorities has been to create a constant state of uncertainty about future revenues, added to the workload and cost involved in tax collection and reduced to a residual level any financial independence local authorities had. Combined with the other measures relevant to local authorities, especially in Housing, Education and Social Services, they have undermined the independence and local accountability of the local authorities. In addition, the boundaries of local authorities in Wales were changed and a review announced of boundaries and functions in England. These changes further decreased the self-confidence of the local authorities and diverted energy into defending themselves against abolition or reorganisation.

Central control over local government policy

Apart from controls on expenditure, the government intervened in other ways in the work of local authorities. The metropolitan county councils and the Greater London Council were abolished with effect from 1 April 1986. While the Inner London Education Authority was originally to be abolished at the same time, the pro-ILEA lobby obtained a reprieve for it and it survived until April 1990. The responsibilities of these authorities were distributed among the metropolitan district councils and the London boroughs or to an array of *ad hoc* special arrangements, including joint boards, joint committees and quangos.[5] The Inner London Education Authority's functions were passed to the inner London boroughs.

Those authorities which survived faced increasing intervention in their activities. Autonomy over housing provision was reduced by the introduction of the 'right to buy', the controls on capital expenditure required for new housing construction and rules on rent levels and subsidies. The rules on rents effectively eliminated general subsidy for housing by an edict that housing revenue accounts must balance. The Housing Corporation has been used to control most of the remaining housebuilding activity of local authorities.

In education, plans for the reorganisation of schools to meet the reduction in pupil numbers all had to be approved by the Secretary of State, even before the 1988 Education Act, which established the national curriculum and national testing of all pupils. It also allowed schools to opt out of local education authority control and gave more financial and managerial autonomy to those which stayed within the local authorities. New mechanisms had to be established by the Department for Education to carry out the roles previously performed by the education authorities. Meanwhile, polytechnics and later colleges of further education were removed from local authority control.

In personal social services, various measures (such as the Mental Health Act 1983) imposed extra responsibilities on local authorities without any increase in resources, while changes in social security regulations increased the participation of the private sector in the provision of residential care for the elderly. The NHS and Community Care Act gave to local authorities the responsibility for the distribution of benefits to elderly people from April 1993. This is apparently an exception to the trend towards removing powers from local authorities and resulted from the analysis of the Griffiths report on community care which argued that social services departments were best placed to manage the community care process. However, their actions are circumscribed by a policy promoting the 'mixed economy' of provision.

From 1980 (1981 in Scotland) compulsory competitive tendering was introduced in the areas of building and road construction and maintenance. More activities were subjected to competition from 1988 and in subsequent years, including services provided by white-collar workers.

These measures represent a move towards direct rule of these services by central government. The reduction of the autonomy and independence of local authorities was not made for purely financial reasons: the government could not rely on local authorities to pursue its own market-oriented approach to public services if they were left to their own discretion. It could not even rely on Conservative-controlled authorities to follow all its policies.

Local policy differences

Local authorities have not spent their time being exclusively concerned with responding to these changes initiated by central government. The past decade has seen some major developments in local authority policies. While, by virtue of being an elected tier of government, local authorities have always been political, the last decade has produced sharper contrasts in policies among many authorities. Conservatives in the City of Westminster sold council houses as quickly as possible, while a Labour group in Liverpool under Derek Hatton's deputy leadership was still building (despite the expenditure controls). The City of Birmingham, under Conservative and Labour administrations, maintained elements of selective education, while no selection operated in ILEA. Authorities have adopted different stances on assets. For example, there was an active programme of asset sales in Conservative Hampshire compared with strong resistance to such policies in Labour Southwark, at least until circumstances forced them to sell land. Differences in policy have produced large differences in expenditure per head on many services, while political styles have varied from vigorous and detailed member involvement (by all parties), especially in the metropolitan districts and London boroughs, to a detached and relaxed attitude by elected members in some of the shire counties.

The political divisions have turned local authorities under different party control into quite different institutions. At the extremes, a change in political control may now make a difference: for example, the election (by a majority of one) of the Conservative Party in the city of Bradford in 1988 brought a major programme of expenditure cuts, including special education provision, increase in school meal charges, sale of old people's homes and other service cuts, as well as some trimming of administrative costs. While central government controls have constricted the freedom to pursue policies based on political ideas different from those of the government, there are distinct local political agendas.

The Conservative Party

In those authorities which have been controlled by Conservative politicians there have been two major agenda items: control over, or reductions in, expenditure and the pursuit of privatisation. These have not been followed universally with the same vigour: the achievement of either requires an active involvement in the face of local political opposition and possible resistance from the managers. Many local authorities have remained under the control of less ideologically pure Conservatives than the government would have liked.

Privatisation within local authorities has several facets. First, Conservative administrations were willing to pursue council house sales and the sale of other assets more vigorously than their Labour counterparts. Second, before compulsory competitive tendering was introduced there was something of a race among Conservative administrations to put their services out to competitive tender. Southend and Wandsworth led the field but there were many other contenders. The third aspect of privatisation is the widespread use of grants to voluntary organisations to provide services which might otherwise have been the direct responsibility of the local authority. This applies especially in the field of personal social services where organisations such as Help the Aged or Mind receive grants to employ staff who are delivering services which are in many cases very similar to those provided by local authorities. The differences are that the employees do not appear in headcounts (thus reducing the number of public sector employees), they do not have the same pay or conditions as employees (thus reducing budgets) and contracts to provide services are often for a period of no more than a year.

Some Conservative authorities have also tried to introduce what they see as a more commercial style of management. For example, performance-related pay has been introduced in authorities such as the City of Westminster in London and Cambridgeshire County Council. Assisted by management consultants, authorities have attempted to set targets for managers and link a small part of their pay to their achievement. Relations between management and unions obviously differs between Conservative-controlled and Labour-controlled authorities, with a greater distance between elected members and trade unions in the Conservative-controlled authorities.

In the early 1990s a theme of Conservative administrations has been a vigorous pursuit of commercial relationships inside the authorities. They have established 'business units' which operate under trading rules and commercial disciplines. In authorities such as Brent, Westminster and Berkshire the whole organisation is divided into such units.

The Labour Party

Most Labour administrations have had different agendas. On the left of the Party, especially in the London Labour Party and others of similar persuasion, there developed in the early 1980s a view of local authorities that they were more than agencies for delivering services: i.e. that they constituted alternative approaches to policy and the economy to those being pursued by the central government. They were to be agents of social change, producing ways of running the organisations which could be taken up by the Party when it returned to power at national level. This meant that their methods of working should be different, involving local people in decision-making; structures should be less hierarchical than was traditional; people should be appointed to full-time jobs as much for their political conviction as for their competence; a vigorous policy of equal opportunities in employment and access to services should be pursued. The boundaries of local government activity should be extended, rather than drawn back; whatever issues were of concern to local people should be of concern to local authorities since they were 'local government' in the sense of being responsible to the local community, rather than 'local administration', concerned only with the delivery of services predefined by statute. These issues included the state of the local economy, although concern with local unemployment was not the exclusive prerogative of the left wing. The attitude of many authorities to intervention in the local economy was not that the local authorities should simply tinker with the market in premises or bias the road improvement programme towards industrial estates, but that there should be intervention in companies to ensure the survival of jobs and to make sure that equal opportunities and good employment practices were being followed by companies which were assisted.

The underlying message contradicted the government's: local authorities were saying that intervention in the economy was necessary either to soften the impact of the recession on unemployment or to ease the structural transitions which were taking place, especially in the inner cities. Central government's policy was to allow market forces to take their course and reshape the economy according to the survival of the most profitable. Even though local authority actions were little more than symbolic, they contradicted the government's attitude.

Employment policies of Labour councils varied: the majority of

Labour-controlled councils were in areas of higher than average unemployment and most of them were concerned not to make a significant contribution to local unemployment during the recession. Some, such as the London Borough of Hackney, went further and followed 'low-wage' policies, which reflected the view that the dirty jobs of refuse collection, street sweeping, office cleaning, and so on, should not necessarily be the worst-paid jobs. Wages and conditions were offered which were generous compared with comparable jobs in other sectors. Even without such policies, Labour councils were more inclined to be sympathetic to the requests of its manual employees than were their Conservative counterparts.

Apart from issues of the local economy, local Labour politicians used their positions to promulgate other policies, including nuclear disarmament and foreign policy, as do local politicians in all parts of the world. It was partly these interventions which caused such a rift between central and local government, and especially the division between the government and the Greater London Council.

More recently, Labour local politicians have turned their attention to the standards of service delivery. They have realised that public support is dependent on provision of good quality services as much as on sympathy for political principles. This stance has sometimes brought the Party into conflict with the trade unions who have naturally been most concerned with their members' incomes and working conditions. The concern for better management has been especially strong in those authorities which have suffered most from rate and charge-capping and other expenditure controls. Reduced budgets have forced politicians to consider how to generate the maximum amount of service from each £1 spent. Perhaps ironically many Labour-controlled authorities have also established more independent units of management although not usually called business units.

Other parties

The other parties have had a less consistent approach when in power in local government. In some cases the Liberals have been inclined to cut expenditure while in others they have not. Certain themes have emerged in Liberal or Democrat-controlled authorities. 'Community politics', or the pursuit of populist campaigns, has been the means by which these parties have gained seats, and this tendency has continued while they have been in power. Decentralisation of the administration has been one route to achieve more local involvement in the decisions of the authorities. This policy has been pursued in Tower Hamlets, for example, but has not been the exclusive preserve of the Liberal Party.[6]

Not all local authorities are polarised politically. In many cases, a change in political control will produce few changes in policy. Also, in recent years there has been a large number of authorities in which there is no overall political control.

Managers in local government often face contradictory messages. These may take the form of defending a level of expenditure which is desired by local politicians against a central government looking for reductions. Or it may involve pursuing a course of action half-heartedly because the local politicians do not support the actions which are forced on them by central government. For example, those authorities which did not wish to encourage tenants to buy their own flats and houses would deliberately manage a poor right-to-buy service. Conversely, housing managers in authorities committed to rapid sales of houses might find such a policy at odds with their own background and training as managers of public rented housing. At local government level it is often difficult for managers to separate the purely managerial from the political. Even the details of day-to-day service delivery are of interest to politicians and may be a matter of political principle. It is the essence of local government that the elected representatives have a right to be concerned with the detail of service delivery, and sensitive managers are aware of this.

EDUCATION

The education service in the United Kingdom established by the 1944 Education Act was pluralistic in structure. Local education authorities provided schools for the great majority of pupils between the ages of five and sixteen, almost all further education colleges, polytechnics and teacher training colleges. The polytechnics were taken away in 1989, as were further education and teacher training colleges in 1992. Universities had an independent status despite being very heavily dependent on central government funding which was provided through a relatively autonomous body, the University Grants Committee and the University Funding Council. From 1992, these polytechnics changed their name to university and were able to award their own degrees without outside controls. Competition for students grew in response to government's plans to increase the participation rate in higher education. Funding was combined in the Higher Education Funding Council for England.

It is difficult to argue that there was a sharp break in education policy when the Conservatives came to power in 1979. Concern over the relevance of the curriculum and the standards achieved in schools had been expressed by the Labour government. In 1976 Prime Minister James Callaghan made a speech at Ruskin College in which he called for a debate on what is taught in the education system and the standards which were achieved in schools. The 'great debate' consisted of a series of public meetings in early 1977. It was accompanied by a series of 'black papers' which condemned the comprehensive education system. According to some commentators (e.g. Kogan, 1985) all this was part of the 'breakdown of consensus' to which we referred in Chapter 1. The shared beliefs in the purposes and methods of education were becoming frayed:

> The process of bringing schools under greater political and central control had its beginnings in 1974, with the creation of the Assessment and Performance Unit, in the warnings given in James Callaghan's speech at Ruskin College 'that parents were anxious about educational standards, and by the flow of DES circulars about the need to monitor performance and to establish the core essentials of the curriculum'.
> (p. 17)

The 1979 government made two early changes. First, it repealed the law which made comprehensive non-selective secondary education compulsory. In June 1979 cuts were announced in university funding, and in capital programmes of medical schools, polytechnics, universities and colleges. William Waldegrave, a minister at DES at the time, said that these reductions in spending were not made for ideological reasons, they were simply a response to the necessity to reduce overall public expenditure. The 1980 Education Act made it compulsory for each school to have a governing body, extended parental choice of secondary schools by abolishing school catchment areas and established the Assisted Places Scheme which is a scholarship scheme to send children to private schools.

In 1981 there were major cuts in funding for the universities, some of them facing the prospect of up to 40 per cent reductions in their grants. The other centres of higher education, the polytechnics, were to be brought under greater central control through the National Advisory Body for Higher Education (the 'NAB') which started work at the beginning of 1982. Together, the University Funding Council and the NAB were to become instruments for central government control over the higher education system.

At this stage thinking was driven mainly by a desire to reduce expenditure, or at least to keep it under control. To achieve this the government had to curtail the powers of those local authorities who did not wish to reduce their expenditure. The controls on local authority spending were necessarily aimed at education, which represents nearly half of local authority current spending.

At the same time there was a view that the education system as a whole should be more market-oriented and should be providing the sort of education which parents, and especially employers, wanted, rather than what universities, teachers or education authorities thought best. Linked to this was a concern about 'standards' and an inconclusive, but acrimonious, debate about the quality of results in the comprehensive schools. A strong lobby had developed to try to demonstrate that grammar schools were better than comprehensive schools when it came to examination results. Naturally it was possible to show that those schools which had selected their pupils on their ability to pass examinations obtained better examination results.

Meanwhile, through the 1980s there were also demographic changes which reduced the numbers of school-age children. Spending could not be cut in proportion to the reduction in demand. If a school stays open, there are certain fixed costs which must be met, however many pupils there are. However, the government's policy was that the reductions in the numbers should result in cuts in spending rather than improvements in teacher–pupil ratios. The spare capacity in schools also provided an opportunity to offer more choice of school to parents and pupils, rather than everyone being allocated to a school. This choice produced competition between schools to attract pupils and thus to survive. The demographic changes resulted in many secondary schools being closed during the 1980s. By the end of the decade there was an approximate balance between places and pupils, which made the need to compete less acute. In some authorities there was still spare capacity at the end of the decade, which led to proposed closures at the beginning of the

1990s. Some of these proposals led to schools choosing to opt out of education authority control rather than close.

Vocational education and training changes were pursued through the Manpower Services Commission (later known as the Training Agency) which used its rapidly increasing budget to intervene in the education process. The MSC commissioned courses from colleges and private providers and used its financial leverage to influence schools. One example of this is the Technical and Vocational Education Initiative, which initially established vocational streams within comprehensive schools under additional funding for equipment and staff from the Commission.

It was not until the 1983 government that stronger intervention was made in the education sector. The teachers' and lecturers' professional and trade union strengths had to be countered before more radical approaches could be pursued. The self-confidence of universities was reduced by successive rounds of expenditure reductions. Many universities were forced to close whole departments, and almost all had to reduce the number of staff. It was much easier to persuade universities to orient themselves to private research funders and sponsors when they had falling budgets. The result has been an increase in company-sponsored research.

The 1983 government also began the process of removing the polytechnics from local authority control, by giving them corporate status separate from their local education authorities. At the same time, polytechnics were made more dependent on the income from student fees, as central grants to institutions were reduced. The combination of corporate status and dependence on fees made the polytechnics more like 'businesses' than they had been.

In schools, teachers' professional and trade union strengths were weakened by defeat in a long industrial dispute at the end of which the government withdrew negotiation rights from the unions and wage determination powers from the employers, the local authorities. A new contract was imposed which gave significantly more control over teachers' activities. These changes were essential for a government wanting to make significant changes to the education system which were likely to be resisted by both the teachers and their employers.

In the 1988 Education Act many of the strands of the previous policies came together: it abolished the Inner London Education Authority (which always seemed to be able to evade central government control); it introduced local financial management for schools and transferred a large amount of financial accountability to head teachers and governors; it allowed schools to 'opt out' of the control of the local education authority; it provided for a national curriculum and nationally based testing of pupils at various ages; it specified those parts of the education service which could be paid for at the point of consumption. In addition there were various measures for the advanced education sector which were designed to increase central government control.

The Education Act represented an attempt to reduce the control of the local education authorities over the education sector, and to increase the authority of the Department of Education and Science on the one hand and the school governors on the other. It also introduced some more market-type relationships into education: teachers in 'shortage' subjects can be paid more; schools which fail to attract pupils will eventually go out of business; parents who do not pay for such 'luxuries' as visits and music lessons will be allowing their children to go without them.

Kieron Walsh interprets the changes in the education system as a transition from professionalism to managerialism (see Walsh, in Ranson and Tomlinson, 1986). Professionalism is here defined as a system of education where teachers have autonomy as opposed to managerialism which is based on hierarchical relationships and control. Any move to establish control from outside the teaching profession (whether from politicians, local education authorities or the DES) implies a reduction in professionalism.

But there have always been ambiguities and tensions between the Department of Education and Science, the local education authorities and the teaching profession about what is taught in schools and how. No doubt the inspectorate consider themselves to be as 'professional' as the teachers, and politicians would claim some democratic mandate to determine what happens during an education process which is financed from public funds. The question of control is less a matter of managerialism versus professionalism than of competing interests trying to establish control over education. Those interests may be represented by the teachers or the government. For example, employers may feel that they have a requirement for certain characteristics in the workforce which they recruit from the education system: these characteristics probably include basic literacy and numeracy, punctuality and a willingness to accept direction. Teachers may feel that these are important characteristics, but not overwhelmingly so: they may seek to represent the pupils in expecting creativity and imagination, for example. If an education authority or a Secretary of State for Education wants to assert punctuality and basic numeracy over creativity and wishes to measure performance against those criteria in a systematic way, this does not imply that 'managerialism' is dominant over 'professionalism', rather that the Secretary of State wishes to take control, in the perceived interests of the employers.

More generally, the changes weakened the scope for educational planning. The basic units in the new system are the individual schools and colleges, each of which attempts to survive in competition with the rest.

In those authorities, such as Essex County Council, in which a large number of schools opted out the funds available to run the authority shrank dramatically. Even in those cases in which there were few opted-out (Grant Maintained) schools the authorities faced difficulties. Limits were placed on the proportion of the education budgets which could be retained by the authorities (15 per cent by April 1993), rather than distributed to schools. This has meant that services such as curriculum support and in-service training had to be sold to schools. Given a choice, many schools decided to purchase a smaller volume of such services than those which were previously allocated to them. The internal market for these services has produced a dramatic change in the way they are managed, producing a forced effort to sell. In fact, the relationship between the education authorities and the schools has been reversed, the schools now being in control.

The next phase of the education reforms was outlined in the White Paper 'Choice and Diversity: A New Framework for Schools' (HMSO, 1992). The Education (Schools) Act of 1992 had already established a new Chief Inspector of Schools to oversee the independent inspection of schools, removing the powers of local inspectors and Her Majesty's Inspectorate. The White Paper claimed this as a main plank in the effort to raise standards in schools and enhance their accountability. Control over the curriculum and testing was given to the School Curriculum and Assessment Authority. Another new body, the Funding Agency for Schools was to control the distribution of funds to Grant Maintained Schools, take over education funding in an area completely when 75 per cent of schools opted out and be involved in funding decisions when 10 per cent were opted-out. Meanwhile the process of opting out was made easier, together with the opportunity to 'change the character' of the opted-out school.

These changes amount to the nationalisation of the education service: local authority control gives way to central government control through a series of new, appointed bodies. Schools and colleges compete for pupils and are funded by a formula which rewards market success. The combination of central control and market competition has replaced local democratic control and accountability. For parents and pupils the lines of accountability and redress are not as clear as they were under the local education authority system, in which there were procedures for appeal and complaint and ultimately recourse to the elected members of the authority on the education committee. Under the system of Department for Education[7] control, the only local people in charge are the headteachers and the school governors. In effect the headteachers have the most practical control over the schools. Part-time governors, often without expertise in education or management, are no match for experienced full-time professionals.

The results of the market approach to education will be dramatic. Competition among schools will not be based on price, except at the margins. Competition will be conducted through differentiation of the schools: the White Paper explicitly encouraged the growth of diversity. What this means is that schools will try to attract (and select) the best pupils so that their test results are better than those of their competitors. Those which attract the most 'academic' (which means most middle-class) pupils will become oriented towards those sorts of pupils and eventually will be able to apply to change their character. They will become grammar schools. The schools which attract less academically able pupils are likely to lose academic pupils cumulatively: it is very difficult to sell to two market segments, the very academic, middle-class parents and the less academic working-class parents at the same time. They will concentrate on practical and vocational aspects of the curriculum. They will become like the old secondary modern schools. Those schools that differentiate them-selves by investing in technological equipment will become technical schools. There is a danger that some schools, especially those in areas of social deprivation and declining population, will go into a spiral of decline: fewer pupils, attracting fewer resources, leading to higher costs and poorer results.

Meanwhile the support for pupils with special educational needs, such as that offered by the Education Psychology Service, will itself be subjected to market forces: 'The Government expects that increasingly the private sector will step in to provide such services' (HMSO, 1992, para. 6.8). The market approach applies, even for those children in greatest need of help. Currently the private sector does not exist in this sphere, as the White Paper recognises. It will be created by the professionals who are displaced from the local education authorities and still wish to practise.

Markets do not create equity. Competition among schools will add to the difference between them and will reduce the equality of access to education. The government recognised this in the White Paper when it defined 'failing schools'. Its diagnosis of failing schools is poor management and lack of leadership. Its solution is to replace the management of such schools with an Education Association.

The implications of the changes for managers are profound. For those working in the Department for Education, new roles require new skills. Managing budget allocation to schools has previously been a task for the education authorities. For those in the LEAS, there has already been a change in role, as many professionals have now begun to sell their services to schools. Others have seen their significance diminish as the schools gained autonomy. In schools headteachers and to some extent governors are learning how to run their organisations as businesses.

HOUSING

We saw in Chapter 2 that the last Labour government reduced public spending on housebuilding. They introduced the housing investment programmes (HIPs) through which local authorities applied to the Department of Environment for permission to spend money on house building and improvement, giving the government control over spending. The incoming Conservative administration used the mechanism to reduce the HIP spending by 11 per cent in 1979–80 and a further 33 per cent in 1980–1. In the event, authorities were unable to curtail their spending so drastically and by October 1980 they were heading towards an overspending of £180 million. Meanwhile, the balance of expenditure was channelled away from new house building and towards improvements.

Once the capital programme had been reduced the only other possible cut was the subsidy paid towards housing costs, and this took two forms. First, there was a general government housing subsidy paid to local authorities to help meet the difference between the rents and the cost of running the housing service. Second, local authorities could also subsidise rents by meeting from the rates any deficits on the housing accounts. Eventually, the government took action on both these subsidies. Initially, it introduced a strong incentive to housing authorities to increase rents: it calculated the subsidy payable based on a notional housing account deficit as if the rents had been increased.

At the same time it removed general housing subsidy from those authorities whose housing accounts were not in deficit. Average public sector rents increased from £6.48 per week in 1979–80 to £14.07 per week in 1983–4. Because many tenants were unable to afford such increases, a new system of rent subsidy was introduced and was effective from 1982. The Housing Benefit Scheme offered poor tenants a contribution towards their rent, in many cases a 100 per cent contribution. The result was that the general housing subsidy was reduced dramatically but payments of rent from public funds increased. By 1991, 4 million people received housing benefit, of whom half were pensioners.[8]

The justification for this was that the benefits were now means-tested and were not given to all tenants, irrespective of whether they needed it or not. The change in rents meant that they reached levels nearer to mortgage levels had the houses been purchased, which was useful for the government's other main housing policy: the privatisation of the public housing stock. The Housing Act 1980 gave tenants the right to buy their council house or flat from the local authority for the first time.

The sale of council housing was popular, partly because of the large discounts offered against the market value. It was relatively easy to implement, once intransigent local authorities had been forced to co-operate. At local authority level, Labour policy on sales had been that these should be at the discretion of the local authorities and should only apply in areas where there was no housing shortage. However, once the rate of sales of houses slowed and the policy seemed to be reaching saturation, larger discounts were offered. Discounts of up to 60 per cent of market value were offered on houses and 70 per cent on flats. Sales through the 'right to buy' legislation transferred one million houses and flats from public ownership by 1991. This represented 20 per cent of the stock which reduced from 5.1 million to 4.1 million in England and Wales.

Even these failed to eradicate public housing because many tenants either did not wish to or were unable to buy, or because there were exemptions in the 1980 Act from the right to buy. The right to buy was extended in 1984 and this made it more difficult for housing authorities to delay or obstruct purchases. In the same year, the Housing Defects Act made councils responsible for the repair of defective buildings after they were sold. This removed some of the risk faced by purchasers.

To reduce the local authorities' role in housing provision further the government had to take account of the fact that a certain proportion of tenants would not be able to pay full-cost rents and would need continuous subsidy, whoever their landlord was. Meanwhile, the government believed that the market needed to be restored to remove distortions introduced by general subsidy and by rent controls.

The White Paper 'Housing: The Government's Proposals' (1987) was followed by the Housing Act 1988. The main thrust of the reforms was that market distortions should be reduced. The demise of the private rented sector was ascribed in the White Paper to rent controls and the growth of the subsidised public rented sector. The private rented market was to be stimulated by reducing tenants' security of tenure through the introduction of 'assured tenancies' and 'shortholds'.

The right of tenants to buy their homes was extended by changing a rule which previously allowed local authorities to take account of the cost of improvement to a building after 1974 when setting price levels. Those tenants who did not buy were given the right to opt out of their local authority tenancies and to choose an alternative landlord. The Act also allowed 'housing action trusts' to take over whole local authority estates and renovate them.

Rent levels were further increased in both local authorities and housing associations. The White Paper claimed that 'whole communities have slipped into permanent dependence on the welfare system from which it is extremely difficult for people to escape' (para. 1.9). Hence 'indiscriminate' subsidies are to be removed by requiring housing associations to charge rents which allow them 'to meet the requirements of private sector finance instead of relying on funding from public sources' and by making new rules for local authority housing revenue accounts which will be required to balance in future.

The 1988 housing changes, building on the reforms implemented since 1981, represented a continuation of radical measures to public housing provision, introducing markets, reducing public provision, transferring assets, pushing prices up to cost levels and removing obstacles to tenants' choices.

Meanwhile, owner occupiers continue to receive an indiscriminate subsidy through tax relief on mortgage payments and there is as yet little sign of the revival of the private rented sector. The impact of the housing policy changes have not all been positive: the 1986 House Condition Survey, published in 1988, showed a very small decrease in the numbers of unfit dwellings between 1981 and 1986 (from 6.3 per cent to 5.6 per cent of the total housing stock).

The period 1979–88 was one of rapid rises in house prices in most parts of the country. The average price increase in the United Kingdom over the ten years to 1988 was over 250 per cent. The price changes were greater in some areas than others: the difference between average house prices in the south-east and north-east, for example, increased from about 40 per cent in 1970 to about 60 per cent in 1986. This made it difficult for people to move from one part of the country to another. The house price boom was partly subsidised by the tax relief available on mortgage payments, which cost the Treasury £7.8 billion in 1990–1.

Owner occupation has not been a safe option for everyone who bought their home. The recession from 1990 brought problems for many home owners: high interest rates increased their mortgage repayments while declining house prices from 1988 reduced the value of their assets. Meanwhile a rapid increase in unemployment and reduction in earnings made mortgage payments difficult to meet. The result was that many people lost their homes. While 16,000 homes in the United Kingdom were repossessed because of mortgage arrears in 1989, 43,900 were repossessed during 1990 and 36,600 in the first half of 1991. By the middle of 1991 222,000 mortgages were six months or more in arrears. These problems made many people homeless: in 1990, 156,000 homeless households were found accommodation by local authorities in Great Britain. Of these, 34,000 had been made homeless because of a court order on rent or mortgage arrears. Between 1981 and 1990, statutory homelessness as a result of a court order following mortgage default or rent arrears increased by 2.5 times.[9] By 1988, 12,000 homeless households were in bed and breakfast accommodation in England, at a cost of over £100 million per annum. This figure has not reduced since then. Of these about two-thirds were in London.[10] Local authorities are unable to meet their statutory obligations to the homeless other than through paying for bed and breakfast and other temporary accommodation. The lack of new house building for general use, combined with the depletion of the rented stock through the right to buy, mean that there are fewer homes available for those people who have nowhere to live. By 1990 the local authorities were only building 17,000 houses per year (compared with an average of over 100,000 during the 1970s). Housing Associations are building the same amount. The main source of public provision of housing from 1992 is the Housing Associations, whose sponsorship is expected to produce about 45,000 houses and flats in 1992–3 and probably 57,000 in 1994. Unfortunately, this will not be enough to meet the need for social housing.

The Audit Commission[11] has produced a forecast of the need for social housing from 1991 to 2001. Their central forecast is that the need for the combined local authority and housing association new house production will be 74,000 per year. This forecast assumes that the private housebuilders will produce about 140,000 new houses per year over that period. If the slump in house prices and new construction by the private sector is not reversed, the shortage of housing will get worse.

A more general consequence is that the nature of public sector housing has changed: in 1971 nearly one-third of the population lived in public sector housing, while just over half lived in owner-occupied property. By 1988 less than a quarter of the people lived in publicly owned dwellings and nearly two-thirds were owner occupiers. Even before the 1988 Housing Act the public sector had become a residual for people who were unwilling or unable to buy their property. The housing that was left also comprised those buildings that were least attractive. Two-storey houses with gardens were easy to find buyers for, while deck access slab blocks or towers proved less popular. Public housing became an even more second-class option. The intention was to make public housing a residual, welfare function, rather than a normal way of providing housing. Lettings of local authority housing are now more likely to be for homeless families than for people from the waiting list in many local authorities.

Nationally, only half of lettings are now for people from the ordinary waiting list.

The implications for housing managers are serious. They are asked to run a business whose primary objective is liquidation. All the best assets are sold, while reinvestment is strictly limited. As a service, housing has become a paradox. If the buildings and estates are well maintained, they will be more attractive to tenants wishing to buy. Meanwhile, tenants are forced to pay higher rents for the same level of service, although they can choose another landlord if they are dissatisfied. In the inner city areas, especially where there are very high levels of unemployment, housing management is particularly difficult. Rent arrears are large because many tenants are either unwilling or unable to pay. The problems faced by the housing managers on some inner city estates include vandalism, racial harassment, squatters occupying empty properties and neighbour disputes. It is still possible to manage in these circumstances, but it is very disheartening.

HEALTH CARE

Before the 1987 general election Margaret Thatcher declared that the NHS was 'safe in our hands'. It was not entirely clear what this meant, whether safe from privatisation or from expenditure reductions, but even those who talk about the 'breakdown in consensus' find it hard to apply this notion to the NHS. Even Andrew Gamble (1988), who claims that the Conservative governments 'threw most institutions in the public sector into turmoil and created deep demoralisation and a permanent atmosphere of financial crisis and retrenchment' (p. 123), could not find evidence of significant cuts in healthcare spending.

It appeared that healthcare was part of the 'post-war consensus', the NHS being accepted by all the major political parties. The consequent lack of political conflict served to insulate it to a large extent from the policies of any particular administration. After the election of the Conservative government in 1979, there was a growing Treasury preoccupation with the funding of the health service, since in 1980 89 per cent of the national health bill was met by the Treasury, with only 9 per cent coming from national insurance contributions (Office of Health Economics, 1982).

One solution was to encourage the development of a private sector. After the 1979 election, a Royal Commission report on the NHS concluded that the private sector was too small to have a serious effect on the NHS, and so an attempt was made to rectify this situation in 1980 with the Health Services Act. The Act contained a number of provisions designed to reduce the restrictions on private medicine. In particular, it abolished the Health Services Board and restored to the Secretary of State the power to authorise the use of NHS accommodation for paying patients. This met with little success: only 300 private beds were added to NHS hospitals. The Act also transferred some powers of control over private hospital developments to the Secretary of State whereby any new or converted hospital of more than 120 beds would require his/her approval.

The encouragement of the private sector was taken a stage further with the announcement in the 1981 Budget that as from April 1982 all workers earning less than £8,500 per annum would be exempt from paying tax on the value of private health insurance premiums paid by their employer. Also, the Business Start-up Scheme and the Business Expansion Scheme provided tax concessions against the expenses incurred in the formation of small businesses and thus encouraged the growth of consultant-owned hospitals. The government also allowed companies to set the health insurance premiums that they paid for their employees against corporation tax.

The 1980 Act also legalised lotteries and permitted health authorities to engage in voluntary fund-raising. So far, these developments have been made as additions to, rather than as substitutes for, the NHS for most people: private insurance companies are still dependent to a large degree on NHS hospitals for private beds and facilities and the private hospitals are dependent on NHS trained (and in many cases NHS employed) doctors and other staff. The use of private medical insurance has increased, from about 6 per cent in 1980 to about 12 per cent in 1992.

The other thrust was an attempt to increase productivity and save money by better management. In 1983 Roy Griffiths (Managing Director, Sainsbury's) published a report for the government which proposed a fundamental restructuring of the NHS organisation, duties, responsibilities, accountability and control. Among the chief proposals was the appointment of a 'Health Services Supervisory Board' and a full-time 'NHS Management Board', which, it was thought, would operate like a board of directors. Management is carried out through the Board and the regional and district health authorities. In Scotland the local bodies are called health boards, and in Northern Ireland they are combined with social services. Wales has no regional authorities. There is a management system in which 'general managers' are responsible for each level of the organisation from 'units' (which might be a hospital or, say, all the mental health services in a district) to regions. Each of these general managers is nominally in charge of the budgets and the management of their areas of responsibility. They are accountable to the authorities or boards.

These management arrangements were intended to transfer control from professionals, especially doctors (who were seen to be running the service), to managers who were accountable to the government. They were also designed to move health management away from a 'consensus' approach in which professionals reached mutual agreements towards a line management approach. The line management was exercised in two ways. General managers were appointed in Districts and Units and had certain authority over the budgetary and planning processes. At the same time doctors were asked to perform managerial duties, especially in clinical directorates. Their clinical discretion was tempered by a knowledge of the financial position of their unit and compromised by their participation in budgeting and financial control processes.

This change was made both to improve efficiency and to allow greater central government control. The search for efficiency is carried out in two main ways. Budgets for health authorities are set after allowances are made for efficiency savings, which are called 'cost improvement programmes'. At the same time funds are made available subject to a projection of inflation. This is often below the actual level of general inflation and below the level of inflation of pay and prices in the health service. Two other efficiency measures have been pursued: an attempt to reduce the drugs bill by reducing spending on branded drugs and replacing them with 'generic' drugs; and the introduction of competitive tendering for ancillary services such as laundry and cleaning.

If there had not been major cuts in spending, why were there such successful campaigns to demonstrate that cuts had been made? How did Great Ormond Street Children's Hospital persuade the public to donate more than £30 million for capital works made necessary by government parsimony? There are probably two explanations. First, resource allocation in the NHS was redirected from 1977–8 onwards to take account of need, rather than the historical accidents of the location of hospitals. Both capital and recurrent spending since that time have been directed through a formula (known as the RAWP formula after the Resource Allocation Working Party which first thought of it) away from relatively well-off regions towards those with fewer facilities. The formula is based mainly on the size and composition of the population. The redirection has not been confined to new resources: there have actually been reductions in spending in 'well-off' regions. Within the regions, resources have been allocated to districts using similar approaches. Meanwhile, there have been movements in population from the cities towards medium-sized and small towns. Naturally, doctors, patients and local politicians in those places which have lost resources have seen their services deteriorate and have made this public.

The second reason for the distrust of the government's claim that the NHS is safe in their hands is that there have been demographic and technical changes which have made healthcare more expensive. Hoover and Plant (1989) state that although Conservative governments would have liked to reduce spending on health they were forced, by popular support for the health service, technological change which made care more expensive and demographic change which increased demand, to spend more each year. The fact that 12 per cent of the population (or their employers) now pay private health insurance indicates that there is a demand for more healthcare. A government which wishes to respond to popular sentiments but also to control public spending faces a dilemma. But if it reduces spending in some areas it will generate opposition, even if spending is increasing elsewhere: if, meanwhile, there is popular support for an overall increase in spending, the government is caught between its ideology and its desire to retain votes.

The solution was a radical reform of the healthcare system. The White Paper 'Working for Patients' (1989) (and the NHS and Community Care Act) proposed that the health service should establish internal markets, especially for hospital services. The idea was that hospitals would be encouraged to break away from their local health authority and form national health hospital trusts, the first wave of which was established in April 1991, followed by two more groups in April 1992 and 1993. Those which stayed under health authority control also have more independent management, while remaining 'directly managed units'. Both sorts of hospital would 'sell' their services indirectly to patients, with health authorities and general practitioners acting as intermediaries. District health authorities have the responsibility for buying healthcare for their populations, alongside a limited number of general practitioners who also have cash-limited budgets for buying hospital treatment. The prices charged for hospital treatment should be based on the costs prevailing in the particular hospital, including a notional cost of the capital employed. Land and buildings were to be valued and a charge would be made for their use.

Private hospitals will also be able to participate in the new arrangements, by selling their services to general practitioners in competition with the NHS hospitals. This is one of the main reasons for making hospital prices reflect all the costs.

This reform potentially solves the government's problem of allocating resources to service providers. The market which is established allows some hospitals to flourish while others fail to attract sufficient patients, either because they are too expensive or because they are not providing a sufficiently high-quality service. No longer can protests be made about the government closing individual hospitals since any which close are the victims of anonymous market forces. In practice, the reforms did not make the government impervious. Health authorities were instructed not to make dramatic changes in the allocation of resources in the first year of the division into purchasers and providers before the 1992 general election. Hence the introduction of real competition was delayed and muted. The London teaching hospitals were a particular problem. The government claimed that there were too many hospital beds in London and that some were too expensive. Previous attempts to close wards or hospitals had met with moderate success. The internal market was meant to solve the problem, some hospitals failing to trade at break-even. During 1991-2 big changes were made as the new managers of the trusts which were running these hospitals adjusted to the new market forces. But the government still thought there were too many beds and set up an enquiry to establish which if any of the old teaching hospitals should close.

The last reforms had the same aim as the Griffiths managerial changes. They were designed to impose a managerial discipline on a group of powerful professionals, especially the doctors and nurses, to control spending and introduce management, backed up by the pressure of competition and the possibility of extinction. If doctors run the hospitals in such a way that they become too expensive, the hospitals will automatically lose resources and there is nothing the doctors can do about it.

The radical nature of the 1989 reforms took many people by surprise, although they are a direct application of the market principles which underlie all the social policies of the later Conservative governments. The implications for managers, especially in the hospital sector, are profound. If they have expensive sites and high unit costs they have to make some major commercial decisions, either to reduce cost to compete on price with cheaper hospitals or to pursue other marketing strategies. Many are rising to the challenge and establishing their 'brand' as being superior to others and advertising to fundholding general practitioners. They are also altering the 'portfolio' of products to specialise in those in which they have a comparative advantage. Managers of sections within the trusts are producing marketing strategies and business plans as if they were running companies. The language of management, which took a decade to establish itself within the NHS, has been supplemented with the language of commerce. In many cases this has widened the divide between those whose job is to provide services to patients and those whose job is to ensure the commercial viability of the units. Meanwhile the salaries of the managers of the trusts have risen and are in line with or in excess of the managers of businesses of comparable size.

PERSONAL SOCIAL SERVICES

There have been two main themes in the development of social services under the Conservative governments. The Party developed a family policy which emphasised traditional roles, especially for women, as the principal source of care for most dependent groups. In fact, the great majority of care is carried out informally, mostly by women. Policy was developed to promote and develop that reality rather than emphasise care provided by the welfare state institutions. Norman Fowler said in 1983:

> it is inescapable that social work should recognise that the great

majority of personal care is given informally and not by statutory agencies, and should seek to maximise that. . . . But that informal provision is often promoted and sustained by the social services departments and the large voluntary organisations. . . . And social workers have inescapable statutory commitments which cannot be carried out informally. (National Institute for Social Work, 1983)

In other words social services departments should concentrate on their statutory tasks and on helping informal carers. Even in the statutory area, however, Mr Fowler said that the development of services should be subordinated to the development of the economy:

We cannot formulate a policy, even in areas as important as this, which is quite separate from the overriding need to revive the economy. The development of social services depends ultimately on the creation of wealth. (Ibid.)

The second theme has been that there should be a limited role for public agencies, even within the sorts of care that are carried out formally. In the case of residential care for the elderly, an early reform led to a rapid growth in private provision. In 1980 the rules about funding for old people in private residential care were changed. The relevant DHSS regulation stated:

when a person is assessed as being in need of such care [inability to live on their own or with their families], when the local authority is unable to make provision, and when there is no alternative in the area then the person is entitled to have the cost of their place at a suitable home paid for by supplementary benefit.

This regulation produced a rapid rise in expenditure on care of the elderly in private accommodation, and growth in the private residential care business. The effect was to give elderly people a 'voucher' which could only be spent in a private or voluntary home. The result was a decrease, between 1981 and 1990, of 13 per cent in the number of elderly people resident in local authority homes while the number in private and voluntary residential care homes more than doubled.[12]

This development, combined with a decrease in the use of geriatric hospital beds for the long-term care of the elderly, constituted the main shift in policy towards care of this group. It illustrates a conflict between the two main aims of increasing the role of the private sector and decreasing the relative volume of residential care: in this case the promotion of private provision was dominant.

There have been attempts at a similar approach in the caring services which are not based in residential establishments. The Barclay Report (1982) proposed that people who need care should have attached to them somebody who would be responsible for making sure they got it. Care could either be provided by statutory agencies or through 'purchase of service contracts' with private or voluntary organisations. Because of the resource implications, this report was welcomed only in principle.

The same proposal was made again in 1988 by Sir Roy Griffith, who suggested that local authorities should take the lead as organisers of community care, creating integrated care plans for individuals and using all the different available funds. Bringing the funds together was seen as the only way of dealing with the fragmentation of funding and service provision. These proposals were accepted by the government, after a long delay (HMSO, 1989b).

The NHS and Community Care Act 1990 brought new arrangements into play for community care. The budgets for elderly people's housing and care were transferred from the Department of Social Security to the local social services departments from April 1993. The local authorities now have the duty to produce a Community Care Plan, which assesses the overall needs of its residents and sets out how they are to be met, including by the private and voluntary sectors. Each person in need of care is given an assessment and is entitled only to that care which the assessor says they need. Once the assessment is made it is up to the social services department to ensure that services are available. The options of the individual in need of care therefore have to be defined by the assessment and by the care which has been organised by the local authority. There were two reasons for these reforms. The first was the desire to avoid the open-ended commitment to paying for residential care for old people. Now there is no automatic entitlement: the local authority assessment determines whether residential care will be paid for. The second was to separate the decision about what care was appropriate from the availability of particular resources, such as beds in homes. In fact, many authorities made an assessment in advance of the transfer of budgets in April

1993 and struck long-term bargains with owners of private residential homes in order to safeguard the supply of places. They are committed to using these places, as they can reasonably predict the outcome of the assessments from past experience.

Policy towards children, the other main group dealt with by social services departments, was expressed in the Children Act 1989, which gave children more rights in legal procedings and set out well-defined procedures for dealing with children in care.

Throughout the decade, the overriding objective has been that of limiting the resources devoted to social services provision. Local authorities have been asked to accept responsibilities under the Mental Health Acts without adequate funding. The policy of reducing the numbers of people in institutional care and increasing community care has not been backed by adequate bridging finance or an adequate transfer of resources (see Audit Commission, 1986).

Increasingly, managers have to operate within market mechanisms. For those people who are running facilities, such as residential or daycare centres, the approach has become increasingly competitive and commercial. On the other hand, those people who are responsible for purchasing services on behalf of clients have had to become increasingly aware of budgets as they balance the quality and quantity of care available with the available cash.[13] They also have to be aware of the options available in the market over a very wide range of suppliers.

CRIMINAL JUSTICE

Not even the prison and probation services were free from reforms along competitive lines. One new prison was opened in 1991 with private sector management and employees. The prison service was then subjected to 'market testing' from the private sector. Strangeways was the first prison whose management had to bid against the private sector for the right to continue managing the prison. The Home Secretary claimed that this development was a response to the Woolff Report on the management of prisons, which was produced after the prison riots of 1991. The private sector may have 'better ideas about how to run prisons', he said. While this is unlikely (there was until 1991, after all, no private sector) it illustrates the pervasiveness of the commitment to competition and privatisation, even in those cases where the state is acting in a coercive role towards it citizens.

The probation service was also subject to managerial changes. From April 1992 cash limits were introduced to probation spending. Previously work commissioned by the courts had been almost automatically funded. Cash limiting implies that priorities need to be set. At the same time a set of national standards was published to guide the way probation work was done and reduce the professional autonomy of probation officers. The third element of reform was the instruction that more use should be made of the private and voluntary sectors in providing services. Five per cent of the probation budget is to be spent on the independent sector. Even the probation service has been subjected to the three phases of reform: cash limits; reduction of professional autonomy; and the introduction of competition.

CONCLUSION

The last decade has seen a lot of rhetoric in relation to the welfare state. It has also seen a significant shift in policy in a number of areas: away from the insurance principle in pensions, away from general subsidy in housing, towards centralised control in education and health, towards targeting and discretion in social security. The overwhelming policy objective up to the 1987 election was the containment of public expenditure. More recently we have seen a move towards market-type solutions in many areas of social policy, together with a new managerial style and a desire to contain expenditure. Managers in all these sectors face similar tasks when confronted with the new policies: they have to operate more commercially, often in competition with each other. Managers are generally being held more accountable both for budgets and for the services they provide.

Part Two of this book is concerned with the development of managerial approaches which are appropriate to the changed circumstances of the public sector. Even if the politics of the government veer away from the market orientation which has been pursued since 1987 the reforms will be difficult to reverse. They reflect a dissatisfaction with large, bureaucratic organisations which have now been divided into accountable units in most parts of the welfare state. While it is coincidental that this has been achieved mainly by establishing some forms of market relationship, it would be difficult for any government to reverse the managerial changes. This means that people running public services have to learn to operate within the new frameworks and to use some of the language of markets and businesses. But managing a business is not the same as managing public sector institutions. In the chapters which follow we see that there are specific approaches to management which are appropriate to the public sector. The differences arise from the fact that public sector organisations have different purposes from businesses and have a different relationship with their users. There has to be a special approach to all the major questions of strategy, pricing, investment decisions, service design, motivation and organisational structure. Unfortunately, public sector management can be a good deal more difficult and complicated than running some businesses. It also has the potential for being more rewarding.

NOTES

1. For a detailed account of the changes in social policy up to the change in the leadership of the Conservative Party, see Johnson (1990) and Savage and Robins (1990).
2. 'Housing Benefit Take-Up', Technical Note, DHSS May 1987. Quoted in CPAG (1988).
3. The services are run by directly elected councillors in 47 county councils and 333 district councils in England and Wales, 36 metropolitan district councils in the major cities in England, 36 London boroughs and the Corporation of the City of London. In Scotland there are 9 regional and island councils and 53 district councils. Northern Ireland has 26 district councils, but specialist boards run most of the services provided by local authorities in Great Britain.
4. Government grants to local authorities made up about half of their net expenditure. The main grant was called the 'rate support grant'.
5. For more detail on the abolition of these authorities, see Flynn, Leach and Vielba (1985).
6. For more about the difference between the parties, see Stoker (1988).
7. After the 1992 General Election, the Department of Education and Science lost science funding as a function and changed its name.
8. See Central Statistical Office, *Social Trends 22*, HMSO, 1992, table 8.24.
9. See Central Statistical Office, *Social Trends 22*, HMSO, 1992, p. 150.

10. See Audit Commission (1989).
11. See Audit Commission (1992).
12. See Central Statistical Office, *Social Trends 22*, 1992, p. 142.
13. As the Secretary of State for Health, Virginia Bottomley, said in her speech to the Association of Directors of Social Services in October 1992: 'authorities will need to carry out their assessments of individuals with care, and ensure that they do not create commitments that are beyond their means.'

PART TWO

4

MARKETS, PRICES AND COMPETITION

Managers in many parts of the public sector are faced with the prospect of operating in ways which replicate management in markets. Even if those responsible for public services completely reject the simplistic 'new right' solutions, they are forced to respond to the challenge presented.

Nigel Lawson expressed a common view that 'market forces' are to be an increasingly normal feature of the public sector:

> The rehabilitation of market forces in the early 1980s was seen at first as an aberration from the post-war consensus, and one that was likely to be short-lived. But I have little doubt that, as a longer perspective develops, history will judge that intervention and planning were the aberration, and that the market economy is the normal, healthy way of life. (Lawson, 1989)

The re-election of a Conservative government in June 1992 ensured that the search for market solutions continues. How are managers of public sector organisations to react?

First, they have to understand the arguments for and against the use of market mechanisms. In Chapter 1 we saw that the pursuit of the market solution had three aspects: supply-side market structure, supply-side ownership and demand-side market structure. Let us examine the objections there might be to changes in each of these areas.

OBJECTIONS TO MARKET SOLUTIONS

Supply-side market structure

There has long been a proposition in the economics literature that certain public utilities are 'natural monopolies', defined as industries in which it is more efficient for there to be a single supplier. This position arises in industries where there are high sunk costs, i.e. exit from the market is not costless. The notion is said to apply to the distribution networks such as water and electricity supply. Here competition is deemed to be wasteful, and other mechanisms, such as regulation, are appropriate to protect consumers from monopoly power (Vickers and Yarrow, 1985).

Few, if any, of the welfare services are in this position. While buildings and equipment for the delivery of education and health services may have no obvious immediate alternative use, in the medium term the land and buildings do have a value, as has been discovered in various school and hospital closure programmes. In principle, these services are 'contestable', in that entry and exit costs are not necessarily prohibitive to a potential entrant.

The other justification for having a single supplier is based on equity: a monopoly supplier can ration output in such a way that every service beneficiary has an equal probability of receiving service of an equivalent standard. While many studies of health have shown that even an effective monopoly does not guarantee this, the existence of multiple suppliers making individual decisions about what to supply would not necessarily improve the situation.

A further objection to breaking up monopolies might be that competition does not promote efficiency in the way that its supporters claim. The argument would be that, even where the conditions of natural monopoly do not apply, duplication would reduce productive efficiency. Alan Walker (1984) has been prepared to assert that imperfect competition is likely to be less efficient than monopoly, because the advantages of contestability would be outweighed by the disadvantages caused by duplication of facilities. Clearly, this is an empirical question, rather than a matter of principle.

Supply-side ownership

Public ownership spreads risk and ensures that the consequences of failure are not sudden shifts or failures of supply. Even an inefficient publicly owned school, clinic or residential facility can stay in operation and continue to deliver services. Private ownership introduces the risk of failure and discontinuity of supply. Public ownership spreads the risk of failure among the whole population of taxpayers, even between generations, and the consequences of individual failures are small for any individual.

Additionally, activities which are not profitable will not take place at all under private ownership. If there is no profit to be made from providing housing for low-paid people, there will be no supply. This is an aspect of the 'market failure' justification for state intervention. There are two solutions: subsidy to the demand or supply side to ensure that the supply of the service attains profitability; and public supply where profitability cannot be achieved. The restructuring of housing finance, as we have seen, has been a move away from subsidised public supply towards subsidised demand. Objection to this approach is based on the finite nature of the subsidy to an individual: a cash-limited subsidy might be insufficient to bring forward adequate (however defined) service for the individual. Publicly provided subsidised supply is also finite, but the rationing process can be applied in such a way that individuals in great need can be assured of supply. A health voucher scheme, for example (as proposed by the Adam Smith Institute, 1984), would produce a cash-limited demand subsidy which, when exhausted, would lapse and the individual would cease to receive treatment.

The other solution to the problem, public ownership of supply, does not produce a complete solution for every individual. It does, however, spread the risk of voucher exhaustion and reduces the risk for any one individual.

A principal socialist case for public ownership is that profits are not extracted from the services. Any financial surpluses which are made can be reinvested in the development of the services. Hence, for example, when housing maintenance is carried out by directly employed labour any surpluses on the trading account may be used to improve the service or to reduce net costs. They are not distributed to shareholders. For a given level of expenditure, the volume of service from a publicly owned institution should therefore be greater than from a privately owned one, assuming equivalent levels of productive efficiency. Again, this is an empirical question: would the distribution of dividends to shareholders outweigh any increases in efficiency that might occur as a result of private ownership?

More fundamental is the question of the sorts of services likely to be provided under private ownership. It may be the case that profitable services are different from those assessed as necessary or useful by professionals or service recipients. The 'new right' argument is that there can be no better way to allocate resources and decide on services to be provided than the market mechanism. If people want them they will pay. If enough people want them enough they will be profitable. The converse is that if they are not profitable they will not be provided.

Demand-side market structure

There are two objections to individual purchases of welfare services. First, the provision of most welfare services produces externalities or benefits to people other than those who use the services. Therefore the user should not be expected to bear the full cost. Education produces a more productive workforce, which benefits everybody and should be paid for by everybody. The second objection is that some people, or everybody at certain stages of their lives, would not be able to make an individual purchase of services which are considered essential by some criteria. Or, they would not be able to afford services of a standard equal to that available to richer people. The solution is to collectivise funding. Private insurance is a form of collectivised funding, but is exclusive to those who pay premiums. Tax funding with universal access to benefits is the most collective solution.

One 'new right' argument (e.g. Harris and Seldon, 1979) is that people will collectively contribute more to services if allowed to choose private insurance or other private forms of funding than they will pay in taxes for the same services. This is because the private insurance provides more exclusivity and therefore a more direct relationship between payments and benefits. Strangely, other proponents of the 'new right' line have argued the opposite way. Freebairn *et al.* (1987) argue that the introduction of universal health insurance increased expenditure on healthcare in Australia:

> Real public sector health expenditure per head of population grew sharply with the introduction of Medibank and Medicare. Not only has expenditure growth been a direct consequence of transfers of spending from private to public institutions, but also it has received boosts from

the effects of heavily subsidised medical and hospital services in encouraging expansion of the demand for health services. (p. 70)

Whether more or less healthcare is provided as a result of public provision seems to be debatable, even within the ranks of the new right. The outcome will depend ultimately on the support given to each option by the voters, which in turn depends on the interests and values which prevail in society.

LeGrand and Robinson (1984), for example, argue that collective funding is simply superior to market mechanisms: 'the method of resource allocation is a source of social welfare per se independently of its output' (p. 13). In other words, users may decide that they would prefer certain services to be collectively funded and universally available and will reflect this decision in their voting behaviour. If this is the case, then the longer-term 'new liberal' project may be doomed to failure. What is almost certain is that if the public services deteriorate drastically, then those who have the financial power to opt out and obtain their services elsewhere will do so, however much their ethical preferences tell them not to.[1]

OBJECTIONS TO PLANS

While 'markets' and 'planning' are often seen as polar opposites, in reality they are frequently combined. Large corporations are able to plan, especially if they have market power. Even in centrally planned economies, prices and markets dictate some goods and services and inform the planning process. Therefore the choice is not a simple one between planning and markets, but of the degree to which markets inform the planning process.

The past decade's economic reforms in China are based on the idea that the balance of power between producers and consumers has been tipped too far in favour of the former: it is time for citizens to have a greater say in the decisions about whether to produce more bicycles or shoes. The first non-communist Prime Minister of Poland said that he wanted to introduce a 'western-style economy'. One way of doing this is to allow demand to express itself through prices and send signals to the producers of bicycles or shoes about what the consumers want. Those signals will be translated into revenues for those producing the goods and into pay for the workers and managers. The reforms started by Gorbachev in the Soviet Union, and now overtaken by widespread privatisation, were an attempt to make individual enterprise managers more autonomous, more accountable and more sensitive to market conditions. The previous regime had been dominated by the notion of an all-embracing central planning system.

Four objections to planned production and distribution are raised by the advocates of markets in relation to planned economies, nationalised industries and state welfare services. The first is that there are no clear signals between consumers and producers. The producers may think that they are producing what consumers want but have no accurate way of knowing: hence, for example, a free dental service may have a 100 per cent take-up rate but since customers do not have to pay for it, the providers of dental services do not know whether to increase the level of services, or whether the sorts of service they are providing are the right ones. In a market, so the argument goes, they would increase the level of service until any further increase would not be profitable and they would provide those services which made most money. The dental customers, rather than the dentists, would therefore determine the services to be provided. Another example of this principle in action is that when eye examinations were changed from being free there was a 40 per cent reduction in take-up.

A major counter to this argument is that in such a system some people would probably receive no dental treatment at all. One of the tests of markets suggested by Johnson (1989) is: 'is it a fair market, resulting in a socially acceptable pattern of distribution among participants?' (p. 5). The test of fairness needs to be extended to include a question about who decides what is fair and what 'socially acceptable' means.

A further counter-argument is that in some cases the producers do know best. Changing from a system which is dominated by the professionals (such as doctors or teachers) to one which is driven by the customers implies that the customers have sufficient information and expertise to make their own informed choices.

The second objection to planning is that the systems simply cannot cope with the quantity of signals that a market can handle. The millions of transactions that take place in an economy every day make fine adjustments to what is produced and how it is distributed and these cannot be replicated in a planning system, however sophisticated. Because of this, producers are likely to receive consistently wrong signals about what the customers want.

The third objection is that there are no incentives for people to do better when there is no 'bottom line', referring both to an unambiguous way of defining success and a reward for achieving it. If people are paid the same whether their organisation is successful or not, it is said, then they may as well do the minimum required for survival and no more. In a market with competition there are incentives to attract and keep customers and to get as much revenue from them as possible. Failure leads to extinction through takeover or bankruptcy, and success leads to higher profit and greater rewards. There is a widespread belief that only profits provide motivation.

Fourth, it is argued that only competitive markets produce incentives to improve efficiency. High costs will lead to failure as certainly as will neglecting to pay attention to what customers want. Technological change is driven partly by this desire to contain and reduce costs. Monopoly suppliers have little incentive to reduce cost because high costs can be passed on to the customer. The combination of being a monopoly supplier and having no profit motive means that there are no incentives at all. High costs can be passed on to the funders, and there will be nobody to undercut the monopoly 'price'. Public ownership and monopoly are blamed for the relatively slow rate of technological advance and productivity improvement in public services.

PLANS AND MARKETS

Whether these objections are sustained or not, public services need to ensure that the way in which decisions are made does not lead to rigid bureaucratic insensitivity and an orientation towards the organisation rather than the people it serves. We can think about this problem by using two dimensions. First, there is the degree of 'planning' and the extent to which market mechanisms are used. Second, there is the extent to which the organisation is oriented towards the people it serves or is inward-looking. These two dimensions are plotted together in Figure 4.1. Critics of planning argue that because of 'signal failure' in planning systems, all planning leads to an inward-looking organisation (quadrant 2). Their only solution is move to quadrant 4. However, intelligent use of pricing

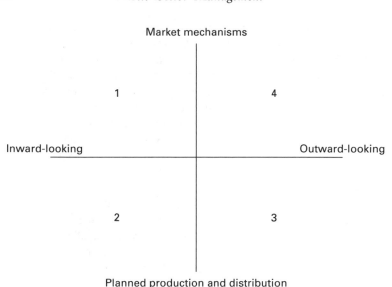

Figure 4.1 Plans, markets and orientation

signals could produce solutions in quadrant 3 which is an outward-looking planning mechanism.

One effect of the 'Phase 1' approaches to managing the public sector is that fees and charges have been increased in an effort to balance budgets. Charges have been increased for public transport, housing, medical prescriptions, dental and ophthalmic testing. The danger is that this pricing policy forces organisations into quadrant 1 in which charges are made for internal budgetary reasons with no thought for the consequences for service users.

Even where charges are not made to final users of the services, 'internal markets' introduce transactions at agreed prices and force managers to consider the same question of pricing.

WHAT CAN PUBLIC SERVICES LEARN FROM MARKETS?

There is no shortage of advocates of 'free' markets. Indeed, pick up any textbook on micro-economics and you will see an exposition of the merits of what is called 'perfect competition' or 'pure competition', and then an explanation of the reasons for which the real world is not quite like the perfect competition model and consists of markets called 'imperfect competition' or 'oligopoly'. We do not need to go through the entire argument here, but, rather, we pick out those features which are relevant to our thinking about markets for public services.

Competitive markets produce an 'equilibrium' (which means a situation in which prices and production have settled down) which has two special features. First, consumers have adjusted the collection of goods and services which they want so that they all have exactly the best mixture. If anyone switched consumption from the present pattern they would feel less satisfied. This is also true for consumers as a whole: if consumption were switched from one person to another there would be a net loss of 'satisfaction'.

The second feature is that production takes place at the least possible cost: all firms produce the goods and services as cheaply as possible because if they did not other, more efficient companies would put them out of business by undercutting the price while making more profit. This combination of consumer satisfaction and lowest-cost production is the golden age produced by perfect competition. It would arise if certain market conditions prevailed: it should be easy for new suppliers to enter the market and compete with people who are already selling there; there are enough producers in the market for it to be impossible for any one of them to dictate the prices that customers have to pay, and they do not collude to fix prices; customers can choose between suppliers and know what everybody is charging; the goods and services provided by the different suppliers are perfect substitutes for each other.

If these conditions apply, the market mechanism works as follows: assume that demand for a service goes up; initially all the suppliers raise their prices and start making more profits. In these circumstances even relatively inefficient suppliers make a living: there is a gap between the prices charged and the costs of inefficiency. Then more people open businesses and offer their services. Eventually, supply increases and prices begin to fall. The inefficient suppliers find the gap between prices and costs getting smaller and eventually some go out of business. This means that supply is reduced again and prices might rise a little higher. Eventually, an equilibrium point is reached where all those who remain in business are making a living but no excessive profits; all the customers get their services at the prevailing price. Investment decisions have been made, both by the existing suppliers and the new entrants, in the light of the likely returns to that investment in the face of the increased demand. If this behaviour is replicated in all sectors of the economy, the whole economy attains productive efficiency (all costs are as low as they could be) and distributive efficiency (only those goods are produced which people want).

In reality, producers do their best to ensure that such perfect markets do not exist. Nobody wants to 'make a living': they want to make big profits by trying to charge higher prices than those prevailing and by deterring new entrants, by advertising, creating a brand name, buying expensive equipment, acquiring the companies of their competitors, establishing explicit or implicit agreements not to compete on price and by trying to protect domestic markets from the threat of competition from imports.[2] In fact, the whole purpose of business strategy is to ensure that the world of 'perfect competition' does not exist. Real markets are complicated. Managers have to react to the actual market structures in which they find themselves and devise their strategies accordingly. The markets which are being established in the public sector should be analysed clearly before decisions are made about how to operate within them.

Let us first consider pricing and investment decisions, and then examine what a market strategy might be like in the real world of public sector markets.

PRICES

A crucial element in the 'new right' argument is that consumers of services should be allowed to make individual decisions about what they buy, and thereby maximise their own satisfaction. They would not necessarily have to pay for all these services from current income or savings because they could finance some purchases from insurance.

If all services which are currently public, including education, health services, personal social services, refuse collection, etc., were paid for either by individuals or through insurance schemes, what impact would this have on the providers of such services? The first difference would be that nobody would have to assess need. Since revenues would only be generated by charging for services, no free services would be provided. If the providers were profit-making organisations, only profitable services would be provided, which would be those for which there was restricted competition, and for which the users were willing and able to pay a price that was higher than the costs.

To make profits above a normal rate of return, or to compete even when their costs are higher than others', service providers now promote brand names and encourage the belief that the products were different from each other. So, 'XXX hospital heart bypasses' would be promoted as superior to 'YYY hospital bypasses', and vice versa. This used to happen to a small degree, as general practitioners expressed their preferences for particular surgcons in their referral of patients. The difference is that now such preferences can be exploited by differential pricing. To ensure that such promotion led to genuine consumer choice there would have to be alternative suppliers of services for every customer, and such choice would have to extend beyond health to all the other public services such as refuse collection services, educational cstablishments, etc. It is possible that choice could be offered among competing providers operating within the public sector. In most of the UK reforms additional choice for the service user has not been the main priority nor the main outcome.[3]

The corollary is that those services which were unprofitable would not be provided. If customers were either unwilling or unable to pay, then no company or organisation would provide them. There may well be certain services, such as public transport in rural areas, which are inherently unprofitable given the prevailing market conditions. Or it could be that some services for particular incomc groups would ncver make a profit. A high proportion of the population of the United Kingdom is in receipt of means-tcstcd benefits. These people have little chance of paying for services at prices which will generate profits. We know that in certain parts of the country housing for certain groups of people is simply not provided and the people remain homeless. It is the logic of the market process that certain people do not have access to certain services. At the bottom end, the housing market has failed the test of a 'socially acceptable pattern of distribution'. It is clear that setting prices to maximise profits and allowing the market to organise supply produces socially undesirable consequences, unless it has now become socially acceptable to have people sleeping in shop doorways.

But if public services are not attempting to maximise profit, how should they set prices? To answer this question we need to decide first what the charges are for. In public housing rents are now set so that the total of rents collected covers the full cost of providing the housing. Many local authorities charge rents which cover more than the full cost, and the 'profits' are used as a contribution to the other services. At the other end of the scale no charges are made for visits to hospitals or general practitioners. In between there are services which have a range of subsidy: public swimming pools rarely collect entrance fees to cover the full cost; charges for home help services cover all or part of the cost.

Is there any rationale for these variations in charging policy? The explanation for the differences in charges probably lies more in historical accident and political expediency than in economic theory.[4] There are at least five reasons for which publicly owned agencies charge for services.[5] One is symbolism: some providers believe that the users of services feel less dependent if they are making at least some contribution towards the cost of the services. In this case the level of charge is irrelevant, unless people feel better the more they pay. A second reason for charging, which is used as a reason for making a charge for prescriptions for medicines, is that charges prevent people from 'abusing' services. If they have to pay they will not make frivolous use of the services.

Apart from these two reasons for charging, both of which are largely ethical in nature, there are others which come closer to an economic rationale for markets: charges are used as a signal of demand, as a rationing mechanism and as a way of raising revenues.

Why should public sector organisations need a signal of demand? Not all services are provided on the basis of some sort of professional assessment of need. Sports and leisure services, for example, may have a public health justification, but it is really a matter for customers to decide whether they prefer squash to badminton or swimming to golf. In this case, the price mechanism is a way for people to express their preferences. If they wish to buy more hours of squash than badminton, this gives a clear pointer to future investment. However, this does not necessarily imply that the full cost of the provision of squash courts should be met from the fees charged and subsidies could still be made. If this is the case, the prices are only a partial signal of relative demand. If squash is subsidised, but cinema tickets are not, the fact that there is an excess of demand for squash courts at the prevailing, subsidised price and a deficiency of demand for cinema seats does not necessarily mean that people want more investment in squash than cinemas: the subsidy has distorted the signal. The same is true for people's choices between public and private transport. The prices per journey of travelling by car and travelling by bus do not reflect the cost of providing each mode of transport. Road users do not contribute towards the cost of providing the roads and maintaining them each time they make a journey. In some cases the costs of providing the bus service are not all met by the passengers. In this case the consumers' choice of mode of transport is not between the full costs of both options, and therefore should not be taken as an indicator of preferences which can be used to inform investment decisions.

So, prices can be useful, but price-setters need to be careful in their interpretation of the signals. They must pay particular attention to those factors which distort the expression of choices through what people buy.

Prices ration people who cannot afford or prefer not to pay the prevailing price for any good or service and are thus deterred from buying it. Explicit subsidy is introduced because policy-makers believe that people should receive a service even if they are unable or unwilling to pay for it at the market price. With the subsidy there will be an excess of demand over supply at the given price and other mechanisms, such as rationing, are required to decide who should receive the service. The results of such rationing will differ from the results of the market process. In the rationing case, allocation criteria need to be established and a mechanism set up to carry out the allocation process. In the market case, people are automatically excluded by price, or they exclude themselves.

Flat-rate and means-tested subsidies have different effects. A flat-rate subsidy reduces the price for all users, irrespective of what they would be willing or able to pay, and the provider does not receive as much revenue as they could from those who would be prepared to pay more. Meanwhile, even at the subsidised price, some potential users of the service are deterred. A means-tested subsidy takes account of the users' ability to pay and can maximise the revenues. In this sense a means-tested subsidy produces a more efficient result. However, experience of means-tested benefits indicates that the process of applying for them and proving a need is also a deterrent. While means-tested subsidies are potentially more economically efficient, they may prevent services from reaching those people who need them.

In some cases, the organisation may choose to set the prices at a level which maximises revenues. The choice of price would depend on the price sensitivity of the customers and the prices of competitive services. Profit-maximising prices can be set in exactly the same way as they would be in a business. However, a decision to maximise profits has potentially serious consequences since the organisation would then be indistinguishable from a business. Its presence in the public sector comes under scrutiny when profit is its only objective.

INVESTMENT

At the moment, public sector investment decisions are difficult to make for two reasons. First, not all revenues are directly derived from customers or are a direct result of services delivered. So it is difficult to estimate the future stream of benefits from a decision. If a company is deciding whether to build, say, a new supermarket, it can make a forecast of the future revenues and compare them with the future stream of costs. It can check its forecasts against previous decisions on similar sites. In those services which have been reorganised into internal markets the same process is possible. A decision to invest in, say, a hospital could be made by comparing the future streams of cost and revenue. However, where there is no stream of revenue the decision is different. For example, a decision to build a new unemployment benefit office is not based on a revenue stream but, rather, streams of activity which produce benefits which need to be compared with future costs. To some extent, internal trading appears to solve the investment problem, by creating a stream of revenue for service providers. In fact, it shifts the problem to the next level, where purchasing decisions are made: all streams of revenue are derived from the purchasing decisions of those who hold the budgets. If they decide to purchase, the investment will be worthwhile.

The second complication is that funds are limited. Capital expenditure is rationed because public expenditure always has limits. This means that not all projects which produce an excess of benefits over costs can find funds. This is different from the situation in companies. If a supermarket company can find twenty profitable projects for new developments, it needs to find its own cash or persuade investors to finance them. If the Department of Transport finds twenty routes for motorways which produce positive returns on investment, it will not build them all because it will be limited by available funds. Under capital rationing the choice of project is rarely made purely on grounds of return on investment; political and other criteria are brought into the equation. If all investments were made on financial return criteria, both these problems would be solved. Only financial criteria need apply and all projects with a positive return would be funded.

One prerequisite for this approach would be a different basis for the valuation of assets. Assets would have to be valued either according to their impact on the revenues of the 'business', or according to their market value. Hence, hospitals or schools which were generating revenues at a rate that was less than their most profitable use would not necessarily be kept in use as schools or hospitals. If a school were on a site in an expensive residential location, say, which would be worth much more as a housing development, then there would be pressure on the company owning it to transfer the site to a developer and turn it into a housing development. City centre hospitals would receive the same treatment. In this way the resources tied up in the public sector would be put to their most profitable use, which in turn is the use most valued by society. In the market, price is the only measure of value.

The investment test of return on assets may simply be inappropriate if assets are valued at their 'opportunity cost' (i.e. their value in their most profitable use). This may be the case for three reasons: it could be that no public services would be the most profitable use for particular pieces of land. Hence all school sites and hospitals in city centres should be sold and turned into hotels or offices. Or prices for services may be kept below their market equilibrium level for reasons of equity. Hospitals may be highly profitable at high prices, but may seem to be a waste of resources at controlled, low prices. Conversely, if internal pricing mechanisms are organised so that the full opportunity costs of assets are reflected in prices, those charges may be so high that demand is suppressed. Thus hospital charges, for example, which reflect competitive asset pricing are higher than charges which reflect actual rather than opportunity cost. One of the reasons for the high cost of healthcare in London is high asset values. These led in part to high prices, to purchasers taking their custom elsewhere and to the Tomlinson Report proposals to close London teaching hospitals.

If it is accepted that purely commercial investment criteria are inappropriate, alternative means of appraisal need to be found. The traditional alternative is social cost benefit analysis (SCBA).[6] While complicated in practice, the principle of SCBA is simple. Future streams of benefits include items which are not flows of cash, such as time saved or reduced noise levels. These benefits are then expressed in cash terms so that they can be compared with the stream of costs. This differs from a purely market approach because it accepts that there are things of value to society which do not have a market price. Social cost benefit analysis is currently out of favour with a government which demands a more commercial approach. For example, public transport investment decisions are now made almost exclusively on narrow, commercial criteria.

MARKETS WITHOUT PROFITS?

Only if we believe that there are values which are not concerned with individual self-interest or profits would we wish to modify the purely market approach. If the only values are self-preservation and self-enhancement, then the market is adequate; if people are unwilling or unable to purchase certain services, then that is of no concern to anybody else. Except in certain restricted circumstances where there are 'externalities'[7] there is no reason for the state or any other collectivity to intervene in the outcomes of the market.

However, there may be a set of values which goes beyond self-interest. There are those who believe, for example, that people without jobs should not have their standard of living reduced to a level commensurate with the market clearing rate for their labour. Many people believe that old people who have no savings should still eat and that children of poor people have certain entitlements to education which go beyond their ability to pay for them. If market principles of seeking greatest profits are not to be followed, decisions have to be based on a different set of principles.

However, public sector managers are not the embodiment of social values. They may not behave in the same way as managers of businesses because they have no shareholders who will benefit from maximising revenues. Managers in the public sector react to their environment. How they behave depends on the structure of the markets they are in, their motivations, and the incentives provided in their particular situations. It has been suggested that there might be a compromise position called 'planned markets and public competition'. Saltman and von Otter (1992), in a study of healthcare, suggest that the advantages of markets can be combined with the advantages of planning and public ownership. In their model there would be public ownership of the provider units, consumer choice and budgets tied to market share. Managers would be able to run their organisations flexibly and successful units would grow. The need for detailed central planning of provision would disappear as individual managers make their choices in response to the market.

THE REAL WORLD OF PUBLIC SECTOR MARKETS

Markets can be introduced in various ways: complete privatisation and the introduction of competitive suppliers (as in the case of British Telecom) is at one end of a spectrum. In these cases any residual 'public sector' approaches to services have to be implemented through the regulatory regime. If producers still have a degree of monopoly power in relation to customers, their pricing decisions can be regulated by a formula, such as a link to the retail price index, or a more complicated formula such as that used in the water privatisation which includes the investment needs of the water companies. Suppliers can be obliged to make water available to all customers who want it.

Compulsory competitive tendering introduces a more limited set of market relationships in certain areas of health and local and central government. 'Market testing', which has been introduced into all central government departments, is the same as competitive tendering. In this case the 'market' introduces competitive pressure on costs, but does not involve the customers in making more choices for themselves.

The development of internal markets in which services are traded within the public bodies (internal purchasing of printing or computer services, for example) introduces a market for inputs. The reforms in the NHS introduced an internal market for services to patients, in which district health authorities and general practitioners buy services for patients. While this does not introduce direct choice of treatment and location of treatment for patients, it puts hospitals into competition with each other.

In the education sector, the reforms of the Education Reform Act produced competition for pupils among schools. Those schools that decided to opt out and take 'grant maintained' status are in competition with each other and with the local authority schools in their area in trying to attract pupils. Schools are competing by making themselves distinct from each other and by advertising through glossy brochures and promotional events.

Each organisation may find itself in at least three markets: the market for its final product or service; the market for labour and other inputs; and the market for capital for investment and for its own assets. The introduction of market mechanisms may apply in any of these three markets. Complete privatisation (the transfer of the ownership of the assets to private shareholders) produces a market in all three areas, although the degree of competition in the market for the final product or service may be limited. Competitive tendering introduces a limited market for final products but mainly produces a changed market for inputs. It has an impact on the labour market through the pressure on costs.

MARKET STRUCTURE AND STRATEGY

Public sector markets differ from private sector ones in that they are designed by administrative rules, rather than established through technological conditions, preferences, actions of companies and government regulation. However, the choices of how to behave in those markets are constrained by similar considerations. Michael Porter suggested[8] that the market structure shapes competitive behaviour. He identified four pressures on industry. The first is the relative power of the customers whose influence is in part determined by how concentrated they are: if there are only a few purchasers for a product, they have great influence over the industry supplying them. The market for coal in the United Kingdom, for example, is one in which the few purchasers (mainly electricity generators) have great influence over the suppliers, as the 1993 coal mine closures demonstrated. The second is the threat of potential new entrants into the market. While firms in an industry may establish a cosy relationship in which they each have a comfortable share of the market, they will all be threatened if somebody else is able to compete with them. Their defence is to erect or rely on 'barriers to entry' to keep the potential competitors out. The third force is the possibility which customers have of satisfying their needs in a completely different way. For example, the Royal Mail has a statutory monopoly for any letter post costing less than £1 for delivery. But a telephone call or fax message is a substitute for sending a letter through the post and is therefore a competitive threat for the Royal Mail. The last influence is the relative power of suppliers to the industry. If a key component is under the control of a powerful company, that company can have a great influence on the behaviour of the firms which use that component.

Analysis of the 'market structures' in the public sector can take these factors into account but the markets may be even more complicated. A version of a public sector market is shown in Figure 4.2, which is a modification of Porter (1980, p. 4). The forces influencing the behaviour of the producers have to take account of the way in which the transactions take place.

Competitor power

The first element is the degree of competition, defined as the number of existing and potential suppliers and the barriers to entry and exit. In the case of the privatised water companies there are considerable barriers to entry, and the chances of a competitor establishing an

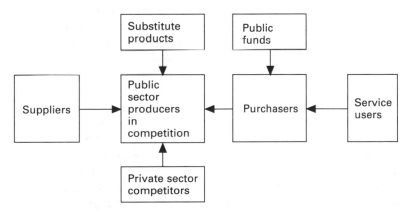

Figure 4.2 Forces shaping public sector strategy

alternative distribution network are remote. The industry is a classical 'natural monopoly', in which the size of efficient plant (especially, in this case, the distribution system) is large in relation to the size of the market. The 'natural' market structure is for there to be only one producer: if facilities were duplicated, the industry would be less efficient (Vickers and Yarrow, 1985).

Very few public services come into this category: there are often alternative suppliers, or potential suppliers, and if there are not the services can be organised in such a way that there will be choice for the consumers. The NHS reforms provide GPs with choice of hospitals. Schools compete with each other for pupils, but only if the allocation of places allows some choice for parents and pupils. For individual establishments an important factor in these competitive situations is how strong the competitors are, with respect to both cost and to value.

Purchaser power

The second aspect of structure is how many buyers there are, how they are organised and how much discretion they have to switch suppliers. If internal markets are structured so that all purchases are made by a contract manager (e.g. a single person in a district health authority making contracts for 'core' healthcare), then the buyers are in a stronger position than if they all have to make individual contracts. The discretion of buyers to switch suppliers is also important.

The information flows in markets are also important aspects of the power relations between buyers and sellers. If buyers know less than sellers about costs, for example, then the sellers are in a strong position. In 'perfect' markets all information is known to everybody and thus all choices are fully informed. In the real world this is not often the case.

The power of the end users of the services is also important. If patients are able to choose freely where to obtain their health care, for example, the power of the purchasers is reduced. If producers are to compete, they need to know where their marketing effort should be directed. There is no point in selling to end users if they have no choice of where to go: the sales pitch needs to be made to the purchaser, whose decision criteria may be different from those of the final user.

Access to markets

Sellers are in a stronger position if there is no restriction on their selling to alternative customers. This freedom is not available to, for example, local authority trading account operations (except in a limited number of cases), nor in the case of schools which cater exclusively for children who live within their area.

The new executive agencies face the same questions. For example, the vehicle inspectorate cannot yet go into the general market and offer its expertise in vehicle testing other than in its statutory capacity. It would therefore be a waste of time to develop a strategy which depended on such freedom.

Market growth

An important determinant of management behaviour in competition is whether the market is growing or not. In a static market all gains in sales are at the expense of the competition's existing sales. Retaliation by competitors is more likely if they face a potential loss of existing customers as a result of price cuts or other changes. In the public sector, growth is not generally achieved by making increased sales but, rather, it depends on a process of lobbying for budgets. Purchasers' budgets are beyond the control of the providers.

Relative power of suppliers

In most public services the main input is people's time and expertise. Some suppliers are more powerful than others. If competitive behaviour requires the workforce to do things differently, the competitive strategy needs to take account of the degree to which this is possible. As the prison service competes for the work of managing and staffing prisons, for example, it needs to take account of the relative power of the Prison Officers Association and its members.

Potential Competitors

Even when the government attempts to make the public sector compete with the private sector, there may be no private industry willing to enter the competition. The government recognised, for example, that there is a limited supply of private operators in social services, especially those services provided to people in their own homes. The 1992 White Paper on Education accepted that the development of private supply of educational psychologists would take time.[9] While there are companies willing to tender for work as the civil service tests its markets, it is inconceivable that there would be available capacity to take on the work immediately. Even in areas such as refuse collection and street cleansing in which there were service companies in analogous businesses, such as cleaning and refuse disposal, there was a shortage of bidders in the early days of competition. Many contracts were won by French companies already in those businesses in France.

The market strategy of any unit which enters competition will clearly be influenced by the strength of the potential bidders. Experience has shown, however, that if the competition is organised in such a way that companies can make profits, competitors will emerge even if they are apparently absent at the beginning of the process.

Motivations and incentives

Not all public sector employees are motivated primarily by material rewards. Very often they wish to do as good a job as possible within the available resources. In some cases they may wish for a 'quiet life'. Others may have entered public services for security, in exchange for lower earnings than they might receive elsewhere (indeed not every company employee is wholly motivated by material rewards). Strategies must be congruent with the motivations of the key managers in the organisation. For example, there is no point adopting a strategy of growth if the key people in the organisation do not want that to happen.

Each of the elements of structural position could be either favourable or unfavourable for the organisation, or they could be in various combinations. We might expect managers to adopt different strategies in response to these different combinations. Imagine an organisation in the least favourable position in most of these respects. Take the example of an individual school whose competitors are strong and are attracting pupils. The service users, the children and their parents, are in a strong position because there is spare capacity in the area. There is little access to alternative markets and the overall market for education is not growing. What should the headteacher and governors do in this situation?

One thing they could do since they are in a weak position as a result of their existing services is to attempt to diversify their products. Many schools faced with falling rolls have attempted this by becoming more interested in community education.

More drastic would be a strategy of graceful exit. If there is overall overcapacity for the existing level of funding, and the buyers are in a powerful position, the most dignified course of action for the least competitive units may be to close.

The opposite case would be a unit which has favourable conditions in most of these respects. It is these circumstances which are likely to produce new products and entry into new markets. A hospital in a growing district which provides high-quality services at comparable costs to its competitors is in such a position. Its reputation strengthens its hand in relation to the buyers, its competitors are weak and it is in a position to enter new markets. In this position managers can indulge in the more exciting aspects of strategic management. They have to spot which new products and services would be successful and bring them to the market.

A middle position might be one in which the competition is strong but the buyer is in a weak position. Access to new markets is restricted and there is no overall growth in the market. One option facing managers in this position is to go for a particular market niche, which means developing an expertise which has a restricted market but in which they can do better than anyone else. A school facing closure might decide to become a specialist music school and gain a competitive edge in that one area. In the United States the notion of 'magnet schools' which develop an expertise in a particular subject is an example of this.

An option when all other conditions are the same as in the last example but the competition is relatively weak is to go for an increased share of the existing budget. By attracting more patients within a fixed budget, individual hospitals are simply increasing their share of a fixed market. They can develop this increased share in various ways, by offering higher quality or lower prices or a combination of the two. Quality may be real or imaginary. One option in this position is to generate differentiation in the eyes of the buyer by developing a high-quality image, including the creation of brands. This is possible only if the buyers are susceptible to this sort of persuasion.

There are two other aspects of strategy which may be pursued whatever the market structure. The first is the lobbying and negotiation that has to be done to maintain or enhance budgets. The second is the restructuring of assets. Most public sector organisations have unused assets, especially land and buildings. By creatively using or realising these assets the organisations can do more, within whatever rules are laid down about the use of capital receipts.

There are no easy recipes for strategies in the public sector, any more than there are in business. It is important for managers to bear in mind the wide range of options which exist as they respond to their changing environment. However, unless the purchasers of services are extremely narrow-minded, competitive strategy is more than simple price competition.

CONTRACTS

The other important aspect of the introduction of markets concerns the nature of the contracts being entered. If there are short-term, spot contracts between buyers and sellers, the sellers' management task is likely to be very different from a regime of long-term contracts and complex contract supervision. In very long-term contracts the boundaries between the organisations of the buyers and the sellers may be obscure: buyers may be involved in quality control in the sellers' organisation and sellers may have an intimate knowledge of the buyers' organisations and their requirements.

The other aspects of contracts is how prices are fixed, whether fixed price or cost plus, or some compromise between the two, such as an annual renegotiation based on a set of agreed principles. If prices are simply cost plus, then there is no incentive for the seller to reduce or even control costs. On the other hand, if the prices are based on some notion of standard costs, set by the buyer, or set as a result of competition, then there is every incentive to reduce costs. The impact of different forms of contract is discussed further in Chapter 6.

SOME EXAMPLES OF THE NEW MARKETS

Civil service: internal markets

The establishment of executive agencies in the civil service (see Cabinet Office, 1988; and Common, Flynn and Mellon, 1992) involves a long-term contractual relationship between the sponsoring ministry and the agency. The contract contains specifications of the work to be performed, the methods by which it will be done and the price to be paid. This is different from the previous situation in which there were many employment contracts between the ministry and individuals, drawn within a policy framework setting out the tasks of the organisations. If the new arrangements are analogous to a market, the features of the market are as follows: there is a monopoly supplier and a monopsony buyer;[10] transactions will be infrequent; the buyer may have a great deal of knowledge about the seller's operations and cost; the input prices of the seller are known and to a large extent are outside its control. It is a very special, restricted form or market.

Potentially, such arrangements could have an impact on the labour and capital markets. Agencies may be able to diverge from national pay agreements and may be able to establish control over their own assets and investments. The degree to which this happens depends on the amount of leeway allowed in the contracts by both the Treasury and the sponsoring ministries. Agencies were slow to move away from national pay scales. One of the early ones, Her Majesty's Stationery Office, successfully negotiated new scales and pay for jobs rather than seniority. Other Agencies followed cautiously. The relationships with the end users of the services are not necessarily changed, again depending on the nature of the agreement between the agency and its sponsors.

The impact of these markets on managerial behaviour has been relatively limited. In most cases no competition was introduced, nor are there strong incentives for change. The government realised this and in 1992 the new Office for Public Services and Science under its first Minister, William Waldegrave, began to press for more competition through competitive tendering.

National Health Service

Internal markets in the NHS are an attempt to establish a mechanism to match supply (especially of operations) with demand. Hospitals compete with each other both on price and quality to attract patients. The market created by these reforms has the following features: there is a fixed level of 'demand' whose total is determined by NHS funding; trading takes place among a large number of buyers and sellers in some areas and few in others; there is competition among suppliers; some contracts are short-term but services are mainly purchased through long-term 'core' contracts. The newly independent hospitals should make their own arrangements within the labour market, both on pay and conditions, especially for managers, and should attempt to attract private capital. If successful hospitals are able to provide operations at lower cost than others and are potentially able to grow, a loosening of capital markets would be a necessary condition for this to happen. In this market we should expect managers to respond through price, quality and branding as weapons of competitive behaviour.

Education

Local management of schools (see Education Reform Act 1988) increases competition for pupils between schools. As funds are allocated pro rata to pupils, some schools will grow and others will go out of operation. Central government, in the case of grant maintained schools, or local government, in the case of LEA schools, will buy school places on behalf of the pupils/parents. The features of this market are as follows: there is in effect a monopsony purchaser with the power to fix the price and, to some extent, determine the nature and quality of the service purchased; there is competition among suppliers, but not price competition; contracts are implicitly long term although budgets are allocated annually. As in the case of hospitals, the impact of this on growth and market share depends on the degree to which the other variables are within the schools' control.

The strategies of those schools which have already opted out have varied: in some cases the decision has been taken together with a 'niche' strategy, in some cases appealing to a particular religious group; in others the objective has simply been survival in the face of possible closure through a rationalisation plan.

The impact is that schools are attempting to differentiate themselves from other schools, emphasising their unique features. This strategy is being pursued by public relations and promotion.

CONCLUSION

When markets are constructed through a set of administrative rules, the determinants of market structure differ from those of real markets which are shaped by technology, knowledge and relative economic power. The structures of administratively designed markets do, however, have an influence on managerial behaviour, but do not necessarily induce competition. Even when they do, that competition need not be based on price.

Prices are used for many reasons in the public sector. If markets are not fully competitive, and if price is not used as a way of maximising profits, then prices are not a good indicator of demand. Nor are the financial results which occur through pricing necessarily an indicator of efficiency or inefficiency. An inefficient producer may produce good financial results in a monopolistic market, just as an efficient producer may make losses if its competitors are heavily subsidised. One implication of this is that investment based on criteria of return on investment will not necessarily lead to the efficient use of resources, when returns are distorted by the market structure. In any case, competition may not result in strategies which are based on the growth of the organisation. It may be the case that managers' motivations are not directed towards growth, or that the incentive structures are such that growth is not attractive.

When making decisions about pricing, investment or overall market strategy, managers must be careful to keep in mind the purpose for which their organisation exists and the client groups to which the services are supposed to be directed. Profit-maximising prices may exclude the very people for whom the service is intended. Investment decisions which maximise the return on assets may result in some activities not taking place at all. In many cases, the reason for having public provision at all is that a purely market arrangement would produce an unacceptable outcome.

Markets, then, are not a universal panacea. Because of the distortions in structure, the motivations and incentives of managers and the distributional results of the market process, the results of the introduction of markets may not be an automatic improvement in performance, nor a clear set of performance measures. Other performance measures are still needed.

NOTES

1. See Glennerster (1992, ch. 15) for more on this argument.
2. Economists call the average return on capital in a competitive market

'normal profits': profits in excess of this level are called 'supernormal profits'. Naturally, companies try to make supernormal profits.

3. The use of contractors for the provision of Community Care services, for example, had the effect of limiting choice to those contractors with whom the social services department had a contract (see Common and Flynn, 1992). In the case of residential care for the elderly, this problem was avoided. The guidance to local authorities on how to purchase places in elderly people's homes after April 1993 said that individuals should be able to choose a place in a home not on the approved list of establishments.

4. See Rose (1989).

5. See Judge (1978).

6. For more detail on cost–benefit analysis, see HM Treasury (1987) or Pearce and Nash (1981).

7. That is, the benefits from a service are not confined to the recipient, but have an impact on other people as well.

8. See Porter (1980).

9. HMSO (1992, para. 6.8).

10. A monopsony is a market in which there is only one buyer.

5

MANAGING AND MEASURING PERFORMANCE

WHY SHOULD ANYONE MEASURE PERFORMANCE?

Even if the whole of the public sector were working in a market environment, there would still be a need for a special approach to performance measurement. Financial performance may be as much a result of the organisation's market position as of managerial effectiveness.[1] In any case, financial performance is only one criterion among many. Equity of treatment of customers may reduce profitability, for example. If a school decides that its financial future is most secure as a selective school it will, by definition, reduce equity of access.

Service quality might be a performance criterion in its own right, rather than simply a way of attracting customers and enhancing profits. For example, the Secretary of State for Social Security judges the Benefits Agency's performance on qualities such as accuracy and speed in addition to whether the organisation has stayed within budget.

There are different incentives to measure performance, according to who is measuring and who is being measured. Politicians may be held accountable for the services which the public sector provides. In theory, therefore, they should have measures on which they can be held to account. On the other hand, politicians place a high value on ambiguity and vagueness. An election promise to 'improve the efficiency of the National Health Service' is harder to pin down than a promise to 'increase the throughput of acute hospital beds by 2 per cent per annum'.

Managers have a similarly ambiguous position on measurement: while accurate performance measurement may be a good way of demonstrating success, a poor rating may provoke defensive criticism of the accuracy of the figures, the organisation's special environment, its inadequate assets, and so on. Individual managers within the organisation may have little incentive to produce performance measures, unless they are paid according to their performance. If a company demonstrates success, this is reflected in the managers' salaries, the share price and reduced vulnerability to takeover. A public organisation's success, for example by having lower cost units, might have the perverse effect of reducing the next year's budget allocation.

During periods of financial restraint in the public sector, managers and workers have naturally suspected that measurement is part of efforts to cut spending or increase the effectiveness of controls. The Audit Commission collects data on local authorities' unit costs of service provision and publishes a 'profile' in which each local authority can see its costs compared with those of similar authorities. These profiles break down the components of the cost differences to help authorities decide whether they wish to maintain the particular difference. For example, if the costs of residential care for elderly people per thousand of the population is relatively high because the authority has a high proportion of elderly people in the area, it may not wish to take action. If its costs are high because it has a higher proportion of its population in residential care, then it may wonder whether its homecare services might not be a better use of resources. While many authorities find such comparisons useful, others see them as threatening and refuse to supply the data because they fear that the measures will be used to compel them to behave differently. This illustrates the political dimension of the exercise: performance measurement is not neutral but can be used as a weapon with which to exercise control or influence.

Any approach to measurement must therefore take into account the incentives for managers to produce and use the measures as well as their incentive to perform well against them. These incentives need not be financial, either for the individual or the unit, but unless there is a reason for managers to improve efficiency, quality or equity there is no reason to expect them to do so.

WHAT PERFORMANCE?

In a traditional administrative approach to public services, the emphasis of management control is on money. Public sector organisations can be seen as machines spending money voted by Parliament or by a local authority. The information systems are traditionally directed towards seeing how much money is spent in each period, and the main target is to spend very close to the budgeted amount: spend too much and the organisation may be in trouble; spend too little and there is a danger of next year's budget being cut. Only recently have other performance criteria become more prominent as accountability has concentrated more on what is being achieved through the expenditure of money and other resources in addition to the probity with which the money has been handled. Audits in local government have a higher proportion of time spent on value-for-money work, although some of this has concentrated on unit costs, rather than on asking the more fundamental questions about the best ways of achieving certain aims.

The public expenditure planning process now incorporates 2,500 performance and output measures in addition to the traditional approach of deciding how much money should be allocated to each function. Even then, efforts to define effectiveness, as opposed to efficiency, in particular cases have not always been successful.

Figure 5.1 categorises the items which are measurable in non-trading organisations. The inputs are the resources used by the organisation, which may be measured in cash or through some physical measure. The production function is the mixture of inputs used in providing the service, in a process designed to deliver the service. The design of the process and assembly of resources are key elements of the management task. If managers are simply operating a pre-set process whose elements are fixed by someone else, then they have a very limited managerial role. Once the inputs are assembled in a particular way, the organisation now has the capacity to produce a service. By using that capacity to provide services, the organisation produces outputs, such as patients treated, children educated, streets cleaned. These outputs generate outcomes, such as a healthy population, an educated workforce, an attractive environment for particular recipients of the service. All this is achieved with a certain degree of quality, which is either defined subjectively, according to the perceptions of the users, or objectively according to some

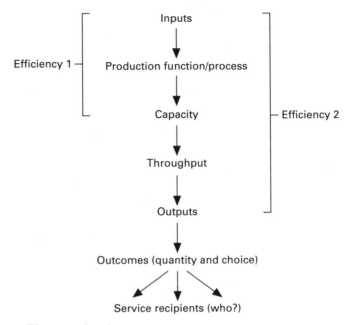

Figure 5.1 Elements of performance measurement

measurable attributes in the service or its results, such as speed of delivery, freedom from disease, ability to add up.

While some of these aspects of the service are more easy to measure than others, we can establish ratios between them. The ratio of inputs to capacity could be one definition of efficiency ('efficiency 1' on Figure 5.1). One could, for example, compare the cost of providing a hospital bed in two hospitals, or the cost of a place in a residential establishment, or the cost of a street-sweeping gang. A second definition of efficiency ('efficiency 2' on Figure 5.1) would be the ratio of inputs to outputs, or the actual service provided. In this case the measure would be of the cost per mile of road swept, the cost per patient treated, per child educated, and so on. Throughput, or capacity utilisation, is clearly needed to be able to arrive at this measure.

A more embracing measure is effectiveness, or measurement of the outcomes of providing the service compared with its cost. In education a common outcome measure is passes in public examinations, in prisons it is the recidivism rate. But which outcomes are achieved is as important as their quantity. If the education service concentrates on producing a high number of examination passes but thereby creates an inappropriately educated workforce, it may be efficient but not effective. This, of course, presumes we have a satisfactory answer to what is 'appropriate' and who decides that. In public sector organisations the choice of outcomes is normally a matter for politicians, although managers and professionals often have an important task in helping to define what these might be.

None of these measures is useful without some notion of quality. Efficiency can be improved, but at the cost of loss of quality. The output of hospitals (measured as the sum of deaths and discharges) in England went up by 19 per cent between 1979 and 1986, while the number of hospital beds available decreased by 13 per cent. To know whether this was desirable, we would need to know whether the quality of treatment was maintained through those changes in productivity.

HOW TO USE THE MEASURES

League tables

The NHS and local government both produce league tables of achievement measured against certain performance indicators. When standard tests were introduced in education, league tables of schools were published, just as tables of examination passes by education authorities were published previously. What is the purpose of these comparisons? Presumably there is a notion that those near the bottom of the lists will be shamed into improving their performance. Those at the top receive satisfaction from being judged to have performed well. In some cases performance league tables are used to influence resource allocation and there is a direct incentive to achieve a high position in the table.[2]

Unless there is some such direct incentive, league tables rely on moral pressure. Where individual units appear at the bottom of the table, all their effort may be put into justifying their low scores, rather than into finding remedies. A recent survey which seemed to demonstrate that some health districts were better than others at keeping patients alive after hospital treatment drew the response from some that all the differences could be explained by differences in the social composition of the population, rather than the effectiveness of the treatment, despite statistical evidence to the contrary. Such tactics may be more effective for short-term survival in a political environment than genuine improvement.

A perverse result of league tables is that those at the top may not seek improvements, even if they were possible. Schools which have high scores on examination results compared with others in the same area feel that they have no scope for better results, even if their high achievement is the result of the social composition of their intake. In Solihull, for example, it was found that the 'best' schools were underperforming compared with the 'worst' when the composition of their populations was taken into account, but that the former still felt superior. Such results show that there may be more scope for improvement at the top of the league than at the bottom of a crudely constructed table. In any event, the expectation of better performance should be measured against the potential of the individual unit, rather than the actual achievement by other units.[3]

Comparisons over time

These problems of comparability are reduced considerably when measures are used to compare the performance of the same organisation over time. If the vehicle inspectorate can say that it has improved the number of vehicles tested per person and can set a target for a further improvement next year, then it is probably demonstrating an improvement in efficiency if it can also show that the cost per test has reduced in real terms (Durham, 1987). Many performance management systems involve agreeing targets for improvement from one year to the next, rather than in relation to some standard of achievement set by external comparison. In the civil service there is an expectation in most departments that there will be a 1.5 per cent per annum efficiency improvement. This may be achieved either by reducing costs by 1.5 per cent or by increasing output by that amount while holding costs constant. Managers find it more difficult to ignore annual changes than comparisons with other organisations, which may have genuinely different characteristics.

Some local authorities now make systematic use of public opinion surveys to gauge consumer satisfaction with services. Now that many such surveys have been done by MORI and others, it is possible to compare satisfaction between areas as well as over time. These surveys can be used to check whether the costs comparisons are matched by satisfaction levels. In the early 1980s surveys were used more as a check on past performance than as ways of achieving improvements in satisfaction levels. They were largely concerned with scaled responses to services, from 'very satisfied' to 'dissatisfied'. More recently surveys have been used to find out what people think about services and how they could be improved.

Comparisons with other organisations

Little use is made of comparisons with organisations in completely different sectors. Occasionally, managers will look at the proportion of administration expenses in total cost, or at supervision ratios. Generally, however, the differences between the public and private sectors are such that comparisons of this type are not felt to be valid. However, when competitive tendering is used, such comparisons become urgent. In many cases the cost savings achieved by private contractors are in overheads and other ratios for which there are direct comparators.

COMPARABILITY PROBLEMS

Variability in the 'raw materials': social class and other variables

One of the main difficulties in comparison between the performance of different units providing services is that the people they serve are not homogeneous. This is also true for companies: a key aspect of marketing for any company is to choose the market segment at which it wishes to aim. Public services are generally provided universally, but because of the distribution of the population, schools, hospitals, etc., have very different populations in their catchment areas. There is overwhelming evidence that the social class of pupils has a very marked effect on the outcomes of the educational process (Jesson *et al.*, 1985) and that health status varies considerably with social class.[4]

What this means is that any measurements must be corrected for the differences in expected outcomes due to social class. This is easier said than done. While statistical analysis shows an overall tendency for educational performance to be correlated with class, it does not provide an accurate correction factor for a specific school's performance.

Difference between inputs

If we try to compare the performance of different units we are aiming to make a judgement about effective management so that managers are able to improve their performance. Hence, it is essential to distinguish between those items that are within the managers' control and those that are not. If we discover that unit x of an organisation consistently produces good results but that it also has the best buildings, equipment and qualified staff, this finding does not help other managers, unless it persuades them to redouble their efforts to get better buildings, equipment and qualified staff. It is apparent that some buildings are more expensive to run and less convenient to use than others. It is unlikely that these differences are reflected in the sorts of values included for the buildings in public sector balance sheets. Indeed, in some cases assets are not valued at all. The use of asset valuation in local government and the NHS is based on the market value, not on the value to the organisation. Similarly, given national pay structures and rigidities in pay systems, the quality of staff will not be reflected in their cost, nor will their relative scarcity be reflected unless pay becomes much more flexible.

Because of this the 'value' of the inputs is not reflected in their valuation in comparisons. If asset valuation is based on the alternative use of the assets, then different problems arise: is Middlesex Hospital less efficient because it produces a lower return on assets than Dudley General Hospital when the two hospitals are valued according to the value of the land if it were used for something else? In the last chapter we saw that there may well be no public service uses on expensive sites if this logic were universally applied. Here we see that this argument can also have a distorting effect on comparative measures.

Presumably, the case for making comparisons of the use of inputs is to help managers make better use of resources. If a manager is working in an area where land is more expensive but labour is cheaper than elsewhere, should that manager be given incentives to change the arrangement of resources to reflect these relative prices? If police forces find they can hire civilian staff cheaper than uniformed staff, they should presumably try to maximise the use of civilian staff on tasks which civilians can perform as well as uniformed staff (Audit Commission, 1988a). Only if managers are expected to switch resources to create different 'production functions' should use be made of comparative input cost figures. If they are not expected to change the way the service is produced, then the comparative reports on costs are of academic interest only.

Intermediate outputs

Capacity is normally defined as the theoretical maximum output of a given set of assets, especially buildings and plant. In the short run capacity is fixed, as additional investment would be necessary to exceed the current maximum output. This is the economists' definition of the difference between the short run and the long run. It should be possible to calculate the cost of a unit of capacity, such as a hospital bed or a school place, or an hour in a swimming pool.

Problems arise when there are administrative constraints on reaching that theoretical capacity. If a company experiences increased demand, it can increase the labour input at the plant to achieve higher output. If it were constrained from hiring the labour, it would not be able to increase output. Hence, a school with spare capacity, such as unused classrooms, has a relatively high set of fixed costs. The unit costs of capacity are higher than they would otherwise be. Schools with more fully used capacity will have lower unit costs. But then, if they are operating with fixed total budgets, even the lower unit costs will not allow the full use of the capacity because the budget constraint applies before the capacity constraint.

If these worries are justified, then what do unit costs of capacity actually show? They may merely be a measure of the distance between the efficient operational level of the unit and the budget and recruitment constraint. Those that are allowed to operate at near capacity will have low unit costs; those that are forced to operate at lower levels will have high unit costs.

Outputs

On the definition used above, outputs are such things as patients treated, children educated, swimmers swimming, prisoners processed, and so on. They are relatively easy to measure, and the Public Expenditure White Paper and many local authority annual reports contain many such measures. In some cases, such as the City of Birmingham, the output measures of the local authority are reported on posters distributed throughout the city.

Outcomes

This leads to questions about whether the services achieve what they set out to do or what their consumers want them to do. In many services there has been a presumption that the definition of outcomes and the way they are achieved should be left to the professionals, who have a better grasp on the relationships between cause and effect than anyone else. If this is the case, then expenditure decisions are an act of faith in the professionals' judgement.

If alternatives to faith are to be used, there needs to be a clear idea of the relative effectiveness of different ways of providing services. It may be cheaper for mentally ill people to be treated at home or 'in the community', but is such treatment as effective? To answer that question, we need some idea of what the outcomes of a successful treatment are, probably expressed in terms of behaviours and abilities of the person being treated. Without such measures, the only judgement that can be made is whether the service is cheaper or not. Even then there needs to be a good deal of clarity about what is being included in the costs of the alternatives.

One approach is for politicians and managers to avoid defining and measuring outcomes and effectiveness and to leave that to the professionals who know best. In some respects school budgets and clinical budgets are attempts to put the resource allocation decisions back into the hands of the headteachers, governors and doctors. Once this happens, and the professionals are no longer asked to define performance, the management of performance returns to a professional, rather than managerial approach. The other option, of nationally determined standards, such as the national Standard Attainment Tests in education, pushes the responsibility for defining standards upwards. Wherever standards are produced, managers need clear guidance on what these are.

Targeting

Aiming services at particular groups of people is important in many services, even when they are supposed to be universally provided. Certain class and ethnic groups make less use of health services than others; certain people have a lower probability of staying on in the education system after the minimum school leaving age. The take-up of social security benefits is uneven.

Hence, measures of who actually receives the service are an important element. For example, a local authority in London had a policy for its leisure services that these should be oriented more towards single parents and women. While the policy was clear there was no routine monitoring of the proportion of users in these groups, so the policy could not be shown to be a success or a failure.

A social security office in Belfast had a publicity campaign and redesigned the office to create a 'benefit shop' because the service was not sufficiently accessible to certain clients. In many services 'ethnic monitoring' (counting the numbers of people in different ethnic groups who use the services) has become a routine measure to check whether targeting is successful or not.

Quality

The main difficulty in using outputs for comparative purposes is the difference in quality of the outputs, but this is a general caveat on the use of quantitative measures. Unit costs of outputs should always be produced, together with a clear definition of quality. This is especially the case if there is a very direct connection between cost and quality. In the case of hospital treatment, throughput and output increase with shorter hospital stays, but the quality of care suffers. Preventative healthcare costs can be reduced, but probably at the expense of a less effective service.

Quality can be measured in two ways: through quantifiable aspects of the service which the managers decide is an important aspect, and by asking the customers what they think about the quality.

In a report on progress in performance measurement in central government (Durham, 1987), there were only three examples of the use of quality measures in government departments and all referred to turnaround times of services. While this is an important element of quality in service organisations, it is only one. *Measuring Up* (NCC, 1986) and *Performance Measurement and the Consumer* (NCC, 1987) contain some useful ideas about how quality can be pinned down and measured, such as the number of complaints received, the number of times a service was not provided, the presence of litter in streets.

The second approach is to ask the customers how they perceive quality. The civil service college recently conducted an exercise with its staff and customers to find out, among other things, the perceptions of quality and what elements of the service were important. This produced some important results: while the standard of accommodation and physical surroundings were important, it was the quality and relevance of the teaching which interested the customers most. Customers also rated the chance of learning from each other highly.

Figure 5.2 summarises the NCC's findings on customer definitions of quality in the health service. What is useful about this approach is that it sees the elements of the service from the customer's, rather than the organisation's viewpoint.[5]

FINANCIAL PERFORMANCE

So far this discussion has been within the tradition of social administration in the sense that the problems are not susceptible to a market solution, nor are they of a 'commercial' nature. What would happen if we tried to apply a more commercial logic to the problem? After all, many of the reforms discussed in Chapter 3 involve the establishment of more market relationships which reduce the need for these esoteric discussions about effectiveness.

Financial targets, such as return on assets or on turnover, can be set for organisations operating trading accounts. A company's financial performance is used to judge the quality of the management, but the result of the exercise is a matter of judgement for the current and potential owners of the business.

Care needs to be taken in interpreting the financial results as a measure of managerial performance. First, a high return will be possible where there is little or no competition. Monopoly suppliers can often make good returns with poor management. Second, the return will be determined in large part by the way in which prices are set. For example, a cost-plus contract cannot fail to produce a positive return. The return on assets will also be affected by the method of valuation of the assets and the choices which are made about the assets on which a return has to be made. If there are large contracts for the supply of a service and a single buyer, then the valuation of assets and the recovery of the annual charge for those assets simply becomes a book-keeping exercise and is no use in managerial decision-making, and therefore a return on assets is spurious.

The other reason to be wary of financial performance as a measure

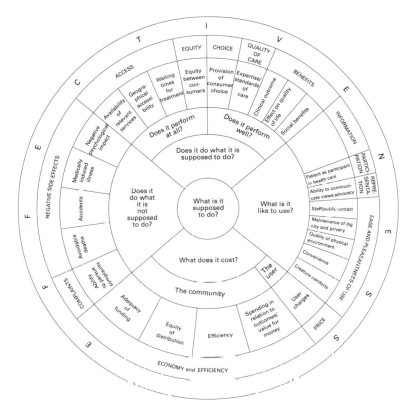

Figure 5.2 Evaluating health services (*Source: Performance Measurement and the Consumer*, NCC, London, 1987)

of the quality of management is the degree of control that managers have over their costs. If wage rates are set nationally, and the number of employees is set elsewhere, the manager has few chances to make cost reductions. Judgements will thus actually be based on control over revenues rather than on performance with regard to costs.

BUDGET PERFORMANCE

If all these other measures present difficulties, what is wrong with the traditional measure: performance against budget? After all, if budgets are produced in a way which reflects the services to be provided, adherence to them is a good indicator that the services are being provided.

Obviously, if public sector organisations are to sustain themselves, they cannot continually overspend. But in many cases budgets are not a very precise statement of the policy on services. In the NHS, budgets are not generally issued from regions to districts in a single statement but they are adjusted through the year as circumstances change. In any case, there are no precise figures on unit costs of services, so that a budget can only provide an approximation of the amount of work to be done for the money. Although civil service votes now have performance measures attached, the fact that a budget has been spent is not necessarily an indicator that services have been provided against those targets. In local government, budgets are traditionally produced as statements of the money to be spent under various 'subjective' headings – salaries and wages, running costs, etc. Thus unless budgets also contain statements of outputs, adherence to a budget is a very partial performance measure.[6] In any case, budgets are often constructed as a reflection of last year's budget, with an adjustment for inflation and for expectations about how much money will be available. They are rarely an exercise in costing the services to be delivered, which have been determined by a policy process, except at the margins.

If financial control is operated through a strict set of rules so that each individual line has to be adhered to, the control process may produce so much rigidity that potential improvements in services or efficiency are lost. Even if it is obviously a good idea to switch spending from one item to another, this is not allowed. Many public sector organisations tell stories about the deviant managers who cheat on financial control to achieve better results. Deviancy is a result of the nature of the rules, not of delinquent tendencies by the managers.

Budgets are normally annual and adherence is defined on a cash basis rather than on an accruals basis.[7] This can have the result that if there is cash left over at the end of a budget year it will be spent in order to preserve the budget for next year. In some cases this might be sensible, but in others it is not. For example, budgets for road maintenance are easier to spend in summer than in February and March. The converse problem caused by annual budgeting is that money may simply run out before the end of the financial year, and work slow down or stop. In both cases, the fact that the budget was spent to within a small percentage of the expectation is not an indicator of good management.

It is worth considering the incentives for managers to adhere to budgets. If an overspend results in an increase in next year's budget, clearly there is an incentive to overspend. But what if the result is a reduction in next year's allocation, as a punishment? The result of such a rule is that the customers of the service suffer more than the managers. In the new rules on general practitioners' budgets, a 5 per cent overspend on the practice budget will result in a reduction in the budget for next year. This a perverse result since extra demand brings forth a reduction in supply!

These objections to the use of budgetary adherence as a performance target apply to different degrees in different sorts of expenditure. Transfer payments which are demand-led, such as social security or housing benefit, are obviously less easy to control than running cost budgets. Budgets for capital projects are in another category, where cost overruns may well be a result of incompetent management. For all categories of expenditure, however, adherence to the budget is not necessarily a measure of competence.

CONCLUSION

The preceding discussion may give the impression that measurement is a hopeless task. It is not, but a great deal of care needs to be taken in constructing performance measurement systems. The first imperative is to ensure that the purposes for measuring performance are clear and accepted by everyone. If measurements, especially of costs, are to be used punitively, then they will create a different atmosphere than if they are to be used creatively to help people improve their performance. Whether punitive use of comparisons will be constructive will depend on the culture of the organisation. When Walter Geneen ran ITT it was apparently acceptable to demand results on the basis of performance indicators and get rid of managers who failed to meet the targets (Geneen, 1985). Whether the same is true in public services depends on the atmosphere and the realism of adopting such an approach. If measures are used constructively and creatively, then all the managers need to know this is the case. If commentaries which accompany the publication of comparisons are written in such a way that they appear punitive, then the reaction will be defensive.

Measures which exclude effectiveness and quality will produce 'targetology', in which the targets set will be met, but possibly at the cost of the relevance and quality of the services. As Alec Nove said, 'one can issue an order – "produce 200,000 pairs of shoes" – and this is identifiable and enforceable. To say "produce good shoes that fit the customers' feet" is a much vaguer, non-enforceable order' (Nove, 1983). Cost-cutting may lead to a diminution of the standard of the service, rather than to genuine improvements in efficiency. This is especially important when internal trading mechanisms are established. Customers rarely buy goods and services on the basis of price alone. They make a judgement about the tradeoff between quality and price, and all performance measurement systems should allow similar tradeoffs to be made explicit. The arbitrary imposition of cost savings may lead to a reduction in service levels rather than productivity improvements. When devising quality measures to ensure that the tradeoff between quality and cost is explicit, it is essential to take into account the views of the users about what they perceive as 'high quality' and the aspects of the service which they see as important.

Equity or targeting of services is an important element which is more important in the public sector than in the private: the private sector can write off sectors of the market because they are unlikely to be profitable. The search for the '3 Es', economy, efficiency and effectiveness, should be accompanied by a fourth 'E', equity.

If managerial competence, skill or professional excellence is to be judged in performance systems, it is crucial to distinguish between the dependent and the independent variables. If schools, hospitals or prisons perform differently from each other because of variables which are outside the managers' control, then what are the managers or professionals supposed to do? The only rational response by someone wishing to work in a high-scoring unit is to abandon the low-scoring areas and move to an area where the social composition produces good results. Managers should only be expected to perform well by affecting the variables over which they can have some influence. To be held accountable for something over which they have no control can only lead to frustration.

The move to establish 'cost centres' in which managers are held accountable for expenditure is subject to the same limitations.

Managers can only be held accountable for those costs over which they have some control. All financial performance measurement and control needs to be integrated with the accountability system. People should only be held accountable for that which they can control, and should not be praised or rewarded for positive outcomes which are due to extraneous circumstances.

In any case, individual appraisals and the overall measures of success of the organisation must be integrated. This principle is not confined to public sector organisations. For example, if salespeople are judged on the number of calls they make or the volume of sales they bring in, rather than on the profit associated with their calls or sales, then the organisation's measurements are in conflict with each other. It is, however, more difficult to align the measurements and incentives, especially when there is more than one objective.

NOTES

1. Market position is here defined as its strength relative to its competitors and customers.
2. For example, North-East Thames Regional Health Authority produced a single aggregate performance indicator for each of its district health authorities, based on patient activity, number of people employed and finance. The indicator was used to influence the allocation of cost savings expected from each district.
3. One technique which is applicable here is data envelopment analysis, which attempts to define the boundary of possible outputs, however weighted, from a given set of inputs: see Jesson *et al.* (1987).
4. See DHSS (1980) and Whitehead (1987).
5. See also National Consumer Council (1986).
6. For an example of how budgets can be derived from a statement of outputs in schools, see Caldwell and Spinks (1988).
7. In accrual accounting, income and expenses are recognised when they accrue due, not when they are actually received or paid in cash.

6

THE IMPACT OF COMPETITION

COMPULSORY COMPETITION

We have seen that a major part of the Conservative governments' policy towards the public sector has been to introduce competition. There has been an expansion of the public sector use of competitive tendering since 1981. In local government the Local Government Planning and Land Act 1980 and the Local Government Act 1988 made competitive tendering compulsory in a range of services provided by manual workers and in the management of leisure facilities. A wider range of services was added in 1992, including professional services. In the NHS, the same approach has been pursued by the government by circular, rather than by legislation: a circular issued in 1983 called on health authorities to subject their 'hotel' services (cleaning and catering) to tendering. The number of ancillary workers directly employed in the NHS fell by 42 per cent between 1981 and 1990 as a result of this policy.

Central government made wider use of contractors since employment targets called for a reduction in the number of people directly employed by central government. It was easy to achieve these targets by transferring work to contractors. Market testing has subjected more areas of work to competition since 1992.

In addition to the use of formal competitive tendering for contractors, there has been a growth in the use of internal agreements like contracts which may produce results similar to those of external competition. Experience so far is that these internal markets in which neither side to the contract has any real choice do not produce significant changes in behaviour.

Relatively simple rules are laid down for competition in local authorities. Advertisements have to be published of the intention to subject work to competition and at least three outside bids have to be accepted (if three contractors apply). If the in-house team wins the contracts, they have to keep trading accounts for each of the specified areas of work. These record the income credited for work done and the expenditure incurred to carry it out. Each year a financial target has to be achieved for each of the areas (5 per cent return on assets, except in building cleaning where the target is to break even). An annual report has to be published along with the accounts. If the organisation fails to meet any of these requirements the Secretary of State may close down the relevant section. Meanwhile auditors have the task of ensuring that authorities do not engage in 'anti-competitive' actions, such as bundling together such large amounts of work that no existing contractor could realistically be expected to bid.

NEW CONTRACTUAL RELATIONSHIPS

The change towards contractual relationships in which expectations about service levels, quality and costs are made explicit and formally agreed, changes the way in which managers have to work. Their performance is more visible, both when expectations are set at the stage of writing the contract and specification and when performance is monitored.

Any change which involves the division of the organisation into a 'purchaser' and a 'provider' with an explicit set of expectations about service standards, volume and cost has a similar impact on managers. For example, the Community Care reforms place the local authority social services department in the role of broker and rationer between the client and the providers of service, whether those providers are employed by the authority or not. The role of social services personnel then becomes buyer, specifier and broker, as well as manager of some of the direct provision. They also have a greater opportunity to ration, by controlling access, those services which are demand-led, by acting as gatekeepers.

The reforms of the NHS included the introduction of commercial relationships. Purchases can either be made as part of a long-term contract or as a series of spot purchases when services are required. There was always a lot of cross-boundary 'trading' through agreements between health authorities, but formalisation of the process and the introduction of full-cost charging introduced a clear distinction between buyers and sellers and therefore new managerial jobs, as well as the increased costs which result from generating and paying invoices for each individual treatment.

STRUCTURAL CHANGE

The first decision managers need to make when markets are introduced and competition promoted is whether to make a structural change to reflect the new relationships and divide the organisation into purchasers and providers. In the current community care changes some social services departments have embraced the split with enthusiasm while others argue that there is merit in an integrated service. In the early days of compulsory competitive tendering in local authorities there were those who argued that it was possible to comply with the new market rules without structural change. In some local authorities, it was decided that the introduction of trading accounts was merely a book-keeping exercise, and they decided to make only those minimal managerial changes required to comply with the law. This implied that there was no separation of the functions of client and contractor, and that the same people were expected to perform both 'buyer' and 'seller' roles. This was especially common in road construction and maintenance, where there is a history of county surveyors acting as contractor and contract supervisor: this became known as the 'two-hatted' approach.[1] In other cases there had traditionally been a separate contractor division.

The new arrangements divide the roles within the organisation into a 'policy' function (deciding overall policy and resource allocation), a 'buyer' function (writing technical specifications in compliance with the policies), 'contractor' functions (carrying out the work) and some central support people and mechanisms.

These new roles imply a different set of relationships within an organisation which includes contractor functions. There are differences between this model and the traditional way of thinking and organising. There need not be a direct connection between the people making overall policy and the contractors, which may either be within the organisation or separately owned. Since the contractors are operating in competition, the control over their expenditure is carried out through the bidding mechanism and the payment for work done at the previously agreed price. Corporate policy (for example, on redundancy) is not relevant to the contractors. If they fail in competition, jobs cannot be preserved. Nor need the contractor be involved in corporate decisions about budgets.

The norm is now that structural change follows the introduction of competition: those units which are forced to compete become relatively independent units with their own trading accounts. In some cases, new departments are established to include all the services which are tendered for, thus dividing the whole organisation into 'buyers' and 'contractors'.

One model for implementing the separation of the 'policy' and 'agency' roles in the restructured civil service is that civil servants will move regularly from policy to executive agency jobs, so that policy staff can gain first-hand experience of service delivery. In practice this is hardly happening at senior levels.

It would seem that the mechanical separation of roles and ways of thinking is not automatic. An appreciation of the details of service design and specification have to be incorporated in a contract. In reality, not all the detailed knowledge of the service can reside in the 'buyer'. Those responsible for delivering a service will automatically have a greater grasp of the everyday realities of the service. The best way to achieve a good service is not necessarily to separate buyer and seller, but, rather, to be clear about the different functions.

THE 'CENTRE': CONTROL AND SUPPORT

The first difficulty for managers in organisations which spawn contractor units, is in deciding who is responsible for pay and conditions: the traditional model was that nationally agreed rates of pay and conditions of service would be applied throughout local government, with monitoring by personnel and finance departments. When part of the organisation is set up to compete with outside firms, its managers feel that they need more discretion. This implies that those people at the 'centre' of the organisation have correspondingly less power over these matters.

The second difficulty is that those elements of the 'centre' which are traditionally concerned with control (such as the treasurer function) should now be more concerned with developing support systems, such as management accounts and management information systems which are essential for managers as well as being useful for financial accountability. Some central personnel find it difficult to make these changes: switching from being a relatively powerful controller to being a support service is not easy. A struggle for control emerges as the managers of the new, relatively autonomous contracting organisations try to manage all the important aspects of their 'business'.

THE SELLERS

I don't want the job if I have to accept the wages and conditions needed to compete – I'll take the redundancy money and get another job. (Refuse collection worker, London)

Dynamic manager required to run Contract Services Department in competition with private contractors. (Job advertisement)

These quotations reflect the dilemma faced by managers trying to cope with running competitive organisations within the public sector. Local authorities' responses to the introduction of compulsory competitive tendering in road and building work ranged from panic to complacency. On reflection, panic was inappropriate in the circumstances, given that the phasing was relatively gradual and that, in general, authorities had already been using private contractors extensively in these areas of work. This gave the in-house teams time to prepare and also allowed them to bid for work which had previously been carried out by contractors. By 1983 the numbers of people employed in public sector road construction and maintenance had actually increased. Numbers employed in building maintenance and construction decreased, but it is difficult to isolate the effects of competition from those of budget cuts, especially in capital programmes, over the period.

In the longer term, there were significant changes in management: costs were examined and reduced, structures altered, working practices streamlined, new systems installed, payment schemes reformed. In many cases, local authorities displayed classic elements of private sector corporate turnaround strategies, such as those described by Stuart Slatter (1984). Slatter examined companies which were bankrupt, or close to bankruptcy, which were bought by new owners. While not exactly analogous to the situation confronting a public sector organisation faced with competition for the first time, the similarities in approach in these circumstances were remarkable.

Change of management

Many authorities felt that the old style of local government manager was inappropriate to the new competitive circumstances. In many cases, there was no post of manager of the contracting part of the organisation: such a role had not previously existed. When more functions were added to the list of activities to be subjected to competition, the need for new managers grew. In extreme cases local authorities created a post in charge of all the services subject to tendering: Berkshire County Council, for example, appointed a 'commercial services' manager to run the contracting side of all competitive activities except civil engineering. As it happened, the person appointed was from outside the public sector.

Finding completely new management was not easy. The jobs were not especially attractive to private sector managers, unless they were in areas where employment opportunities were scarce. Nevertheless, the newly appointed managers found it easier to introduce radical changes than had incumbent managers and in some cases were able to introduce their own, new management team.

Stronger financial control

Traditionally, financial control had been a matter of keeping expenditure within a previously agreed budget for the organisation as a whole. When trading accounts were introduced, expenditure had to be controlled not just against budget, but against the revenue being generated by the work carried out. This required new financial control mechanisms. In the meantime the managers at the top of the organisation often had to take emergency measures. In one case (in the City of Glasgow Building Works Department) the new manager required that all payments of £1,000+ should be authorised by him personally until new controls were installed. Once new mechanisms were established, detailed control could again be exercised by more junior managers.

Product-market reorientation

The new competitive situation required market analysis to see whether success was possible. In many cases analysis revealed that success was highly unlikely in certain areas of work, where the competing contractors had access to cheaper labour and much lower overheads. Some authorities decided to withdraw from these markets immediately. In other cases, management decided to add activities and customers to their portfolios to compensate for the possible and actual loss of business through competition. Parallel experience in the health service shows that some areas, laundries, for example, actually expanded their customer base. Because of restrictions on the access to markets (local authorities are not allowed to trade with the private sector) the next logical step was privatisation, or the establishment of a company to work for the potential customers in the private sector. There have been many examples of buyouts by managers who think that there are more opportunities in the private sector. Some have been of dubious legality as people set up companies while still employed by the public authority. Others have received preferential treatment from their sponsoring organisation to make sure that they succeed. Few have been entirely successful.

Improved marketing

While these efforts were made to identify new customers, many people recognised the need to present a better face to the existing customers, since they were no longer a captive market. There had been some antagonism between, for instance, housing managers and managers of direct labour organisations. Much effort went into logos, brochures, vehicle liveries and public relations campaigns. A secondary effect of this was that a different image was also presented to the public, even though the primary effort was to convince the 'buyers' in the client departments of the organisation. To make such campaigns convincing, the services also had to be improved in reality. There is no doubt that genuine efforts have been made to improve services in response to users and clients, as well as to reduce costs.

Similar developments occurred in the executive agencies established in the civil service. Companies House produced a new logo, complete with the slogan 'Companies House Means Business', to represent its new commercial approach to its services. The Property Services Agency proclaimed that it is 'Building for the Nation'. Such promotion was insufficient to prevent it from being privatised, most being transferred to Tarmac with a payment of £500 million to cover future redundancy costs.

Cost reduction

Where it was obvious that prices were uncompetitive, heroic efforts were made to improve costs. Some of these were book-keeping exercises involving the reallocation of overheads, but many were genuine and successful. In the case of building maintenance work, cost reduction and service improvement often involved changes in time-honoured working practices. Tradespeople were persuaded to cross demarcation lines (plumbers doing some plastering, glaziers doing painting) to speed up the work. It also involved management rethinking how work was organised: better delivery of materials and equipment; more streamlined work organisation; less reliance on bonus schemes as a work control mechanism and more use of direct supervision. These changes have generally been achieved with co-operation from trades unions both at shop steward and official level. The introduction of competition went a long way towards uniting the management and the workers against the external threat.

Asset reduction

Once a target of return on assets was established, and once asset use was charged to the accounts through depreciation, many departments rationalised their asset holdings. This particularly applied to depots: within six months of the introduction of the 1980 legislation 17 per cent of shire districts and 50 per cent of metropolitan districts had disposed of depots to reduce the asset base (see Flynn and Walsh, 1982).

In other cases, administrative changes were made so that assets appeared elsewhere in the balance sheets and were leased to the trading account operations when they were needed. The 1988 legislation did not result in such a focus on assets because contracts were written whereby the contractors supplied labour and management and possibly plant as well, but were expected to operate from local authority depots. So, even if depots were on very expensive land, this opportunity cost was not taken into account when the competition occurred.

Investment

In some cases investments were made in different technologies to make the organisations more competitive. Vehicles were replaced with more suitable fleets; radio systems were installed; computers were bought to improve ordering and control; ladders which could be safely used by one person instead of two were purchased. In the NHS, competition for catering contracts produced a switch towards 'cook–chill' catering instead of freshly prepared produce. Buildings cleaning operations were forced to examine the best available machines and supplies.

These changes in the way in which the trading organisations are managed have ensured the survival of the vast majority of them. In the first round of competition for local authority refuse disposal, street cleansing and buildings cleaning work, almost all the contracts were awarded to the in-house teams.

When the in-house bids are successful, the management of the in-house team differs from the old regime in two further respects. Service standards are specified in the contract and there is probably a contract supervisor to ensure that they are adhered to and that the price is fixed. Hence management attention is focused on performance and price. In the absence of a detailed specification of service standards the 'old' management focus was on producing an ill-defined service within a cost limit. If expected unit costs were being exceeded, then it was always an option to stay within the budget by reducing the volume or quality of service. If housing repair budgets were being broken before the end of the financial year, then some variable costs could be saved by reducing the volume of repairs, for example. In the new regime the volume and the unit costs, or prices, can be specified in the contract and demanded by the client. The manager of the in-house operation can only affect the department's destiny within the contract. The client, on the other hand, does not have the flexibility to cut budgets without being in breach of contract.

Managers who run trading accounts concentrate on the revenue side of the account, as well as on the expenses. If they know that the quality and quantity of work performed will be monitored by the client, they need to ensure that the specification is adhered to; otherwise bills will not be paid. They will also be very careful to ensure that no work is carried out unless income is credited in exchange. This can lead to a less flexible attitude among managers. It can even lead to practices which derive directly from an exclusive focus on profit. Contractors aim to generate as much profit as possible. When public sector managers are given a profit target, their actions may also be focused on this to the exclusion of quality and public service. Whether the contractors are privately or publicly owned, they need to be supervised by the buyer's side to ensure that they meet the specifications.

THE WORKERS

When there is a strict division of the organisation into buyers and sellers or contractors and clients, the use of employment policies as part of social policy becomes more difficult to sustain, for example if an authority has a 'low-wage' agreement by which manual workers are guaranteed a minimum weekly wage which is in excess of that paid by private contractors. One member said: 'I did not get elected to local government office to cut the wages of low-paid workers.' Conditions of service are as much a part of politics as service delivery. However, the same member agreed that defining service standards and ensuring value for money are also an important aspect of the members' role. The change introduced by competitive tendering is that the members can no longer control the pay of their employees, or those of the employees of the contractors. The competition process determines the sums of money available for pay. In many cases the most competitive strategy was to adopt a high-wage and high-productivity agreement. While this increased an individual worker's pay, it reduced unit costs of output while decreasing the size of the workforce. In the case of women workers the opposite has been true. The Equal Opportunities Commission reported in 1992 that women's take-home pay in cleaning had been reduced as a result of competitive tendering, while men's pay had either improved or stayed the same.

Of parallel importance in central government was the Treasury's concern that when the executive agencies set their own remuneration levels, Treasury control of the central bargaining process would be lost. Some people in the Treasury feared that the autonomous agencies will be too generous with their salaries. Others felt that regional differentials reduce average pay. Agencies were introduced into the civil service, along with more flexibility in civil service pay, increasing regional differences in pay, premiums for people in occupations in high demand and merit pay for good performance.

Where competition is introduced, national pay agreements can only be sustained if there is no local competitor able to pay less than the nationally agreed rates. In effect, wage rates (and other aspects of cost) are set in relation to the state of the local labour market. This also applies to conditions of service. Standby payments for school cleaners during school holidays, for cxample, were an early victim of the introduction of competition for school cleaning.

In certain jobs, the workforce changes its character. In some trades (such as building trades and motor fitting) a large proportion of the employees will be older workers who are satisfied with steady but not spectacular earnings. If competition leads to the need for high speed and high productivity, possibly combined with high earnings, a different sort of employee is more likely to succeed.

Union membership levels are sustained only if the companies which win the contracts are unionised and employ similar numbers of people as under the directly employed arrangements. Cost reductions are generally made by reducing the size of the workforce, and unionisation rates in areas such as cleaning are low. The implications for unions such as NUPE, a large proportion of whose members are manual workers in the local authority sector, and especially in education, were serious as national bargaining was eroded and membership declined, leading to a merger with the main NHS manual workers union, the Confederation of Health Service Employees.[2]

THE BUYERS

Once the decision is made to write a contract to supply a service, the organisation requires somebody to act as a buyer. In local authorities, one interpretation of the constitutional position would be that the elected members 'buy' the services, using money from ratepayers and grants from central government. The 'sellers' are the officers and workers in the authority and any contractors who might be involved in service provision. This is an idealisation of the actual relationship, in which the functions of buyer and seller are connected. Elected members are in reality involved in the process as employers, buying people's time and effort, as well as specifying and buying services. They are often concerned with the details of terms and conditions of service of the employees, sometimes in preference to the role of representative of the people as consumers of services. Indeed, in the case of employers of low-paid workers, social policy is implemented through paying decent wages and employing people from disadvantaged groups, or employing people in a particular way, such as through job sharing. Privatising the employment relationship by the enforced use of contractors is an attempt to prevent the use of employment in such a way. The competitive tendering legislation specifically excludes the use of such non-commercial matters as criteria for selecting contracts with private companies.

A further change is the need to develop the skills of the people in the 'buyer' function. Local authorities have traditionally held contracts with a range of suppliers, but these have been predominantly in the areas of civil engineering and building contracting and the supply of materials. Once services are subject to a contracting regime, new skills are required in writing service specifications and monitoring performance.

Once the contract has been awarded and is running, the buyer's task is to check that the specification has been met, and to follow various default procedures to take corrective action if it has not. This may appear to be superficially similar to managing an employment contract. The difference is that employment contracts are, in general, less specific than service contracts, and negotiation of changes is carried out through established negotiation and consultation procedures, all of which are of a different form when contractors are employed. The manager/buyers have to learn the new forms, while the contractors will have a head start in negotiation skills with clients. Penalties for default are not the only way of ensuring quality. In many cases the contractor, whether in-house or private company, will need help from the buyer in making improvements to the service. This will be especially important in cases where the best managers are separated from the direct management of the workforce and posted to a 'client' section.

INNOVATION AND PROMOTION

Once a contract has been awarded, changes to the method of service delivery will be possible only after renegotiation. Suggestions for changes are more likely to result from the service providers' daily contact with the customers than with a 'head office' policy-making process.

Hence, new ways of working which allow innovation have to be established. In the field of personal social services, many voluntary and charitable organisations do not wish to work as contractors but prefer to continue in their existing roles. In many cases, such as the hospice movement, major innovations have come from the voluntary sector.

There may not be a voluntary or private sector which is able to do the work. In the first round of local authority contracting out for refuse and street cleansing services, many contracts were uncontested. If community care organisations are expected to provide alternatives to local authority social services departments, someone will have to set them up. Unless they are potentially profitable they will not be developed. Recent experience in the private home-care sector suggests that profit margins are small, the client group has limited funds and competition is quite strong in some areas. The development of contracts between social services departments and private home-care companies needs to take account of the fragile state of some of the businesses.

It can be seen from this discussion that the new relationships imply a fairly complicated structure. The 'buyers' may be involved both in the formulation of policy and in development and quality control among the 'contractors'. Meanwhile, if the policy-makers and buyers wish to get feedback from the users or customers, they have to make arrangements to do so directly or else rely on the contractors to provide it. These connections are illustrated in Figure 6.1.

ORGANISATIONAL BOUNDARIES AND COSTS

The cost of the process is not negligible. One report (SOLACE/ LGTB, 1988) suggests that: 'Contracts let so far have usually shown savings greater than the additional costs of going out to tender and monitoring contract performance' (p. 10). This echoes the views expressed in the DOE's consultation paper, that in the long run benefits will outweigh extra costs.

The introduction of competition has an impact on costs of services. For example, Domberger *et al.* (1986) showed that refuse collection costs are reduced by the application of the tendering process, whoever wins. Walsh (1991) also showed that the competition process produced lower costs. It is likely that such reductions are achieved by a combination of labour utilisation rates (people work longer), labour productivity (people work harder), working methods (work is better organised) and wage rates (people are paid less). These are in turn a result of greater managerial control of the work process, combined with diminished union control. However, it is

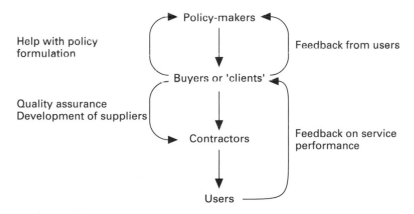

Figure 6.1 The contracting organisation

difficult to separate these effects from the overall balance of supply and demand for labour.

While competition can reduce the direct costs of providing services, it also introduces new indirect costs. The buyer side of the organisation needs to employ people to specify, supervise, monitor and police the contractors.

The establishment of contracts to carry out work, rather than employing labour directly, changes the boundary of the organisation. Coase (1937) wrote the most influential article on the determinants of the boundaries of firms through the use of contracts for supply of goods. The costs of transacting with other organisations, and the limitations of information in markets, are cited as the determinants of the boundaries of firms.

Such an analysis has been extensively developed by Williamson (1975) to provide a general theory of organisational boundaries based on transaction cost analysis. To summarise the Williamson position: organisations which are engaged in recurrent purchases or contracts will purchase goods and services through spot contracts if there are many suppliers and if the 'contract' involved in the purchase is simple. Whether the organisation enters into long-term contracts or internalises the production of a good or service will depend on the state of the following variables:

1. The number of contractors in the field.
2. The degree of collusion between them.
3. The frequency of competition.
4. The complexity of the contracts and the methods of supervision.

If there is a large number of potential suppliers, the buyer is less likely to face a supplier which is more powerful than itself. Genuine competition among suppliers should put the buyers in a more powerful position. Even if there are many suppliers, there is often a chance that they will collude to fix prices or to reduce the numbers who tender for any particular contract. Also, if purchases are made frequently, there is a greater opportunity to test market prices. Williamson also argues that if the mechanisms for writing and supervising contracts are complex, this increases the cost of contracting. If the contracts are very complex to write and monitor, and/or if there are few suppliers, there may be an advantage in internalising the transactions by substituting an employment contract for a contract to supply. This can be achieved either by purchasing the supplier or by employing people to provide the same service. The impact of the two main variables (number of suppliers and complexity of contract) is summarised in Figure 6.2. Williamson argues that firms will reach an equilibrium position in which the costs of transactions are minimised. If the costs of making many spot contracts are high, the organisation will tend to enter long-term relational contracts with suppliers. If the costs of writing and maintaining those contracts are high, there will be a tendency to internalise. The boundary of the organisation will be established in such a way that the type and length of contract and the organisational boundary will reflect contracting costs and not other matters such as technology.

It is apparent that the competition process can produce a step reduction in costs or a one-off reduction. If the market were allowed to operate unimpeded, what would happen next is that authorities

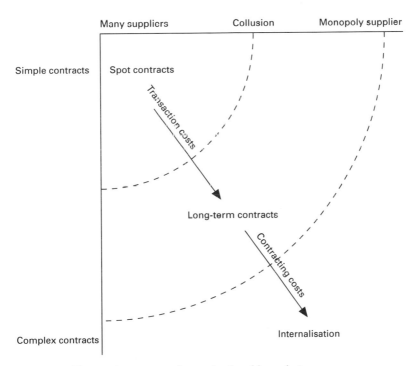

Figure 6.2 Transaction costs and organisational boundaries

would be allowed to arrive at the position where additional in-house supervision costs combined with the costs of opportunism, and collusion or small numbers on the supply side did not exceed these cost savings.[3]

The legislation on compulsory competition ensures that a new organisational equilibrium does not occur, and that the competition process will be repeated *ad infinitum*, on the assumption that the savings will outweigh the costs. In addition, a continuous process of competitive tendering prevents the establishment of relationships with suppliers in which matters such as quality assurance and the development and redesign of services can be approached mutually. Such relationships require trust on both sides, and can only be established over long periods. The use of competition and a contractual style of relationship leads to inflexibility.

CONCLUSION

There has always been close co-operation between contractors and public sector organisations. The way in which competition has been organised among contractors and the way in which contracts have been written has varied. Chadwick (1859, quoted in Crain and Ekelund, 1976) made the distinction between 'competition for the field' and 'competition within the field' of activity.

Chadwick's analysis was that there was a widespread use of competition 'for the field' of activity in Europe but very little in Britain. The result of these differences is that there has been relatively little experience of the development of companies for the provision of public services in Britain. Recent bids by French public utility companies for British water companies may foreshadow greater European involvement in British public sector provision as the European companies are allowed to expand their activities in Britain. French water companies are already strongly represented outside France; for example, they run the entire water supply system in Macau.

These considerations help to situate the recent and proposed developments in contracting out. There has been some attempt to introduce competition for the field. The permission for Mercury to compete with Telecom and the reaffiramtion of the right to supply to the national grid in the privatisation of electricity are examples of competition for the field. However, all the legislation on competitive tendering promotes competition within the field. The experience has mainly been of competition by contractors being given relatively short-term contracts to carry out specific works or provide specific services under the supervision of public authorities. The relationship between the public agency and the service recipient remains the same. There is collectively financed provision with no payment by the recipient at the point of delivery.

More radical changes, introducing competition for rather than within the field, is introduced by the privatisation of electricity generation, with companies competing for the right to supply electricity to the grid, and the possible privatisation of British Rail, in which one option is that companies could compete for a long-term right to supply rail services on the rail network. In these cases, public sector involvement is one of regulation, especially if the resultant company is in a new monopoly position.

The overt objective for competitive tendering and contracting is increased efficiency. This will be achieved by reducing employment and increasing productivity, which will achieve two subsidiary objectives, i.e. to reduce the number of people employed by the public sector and to curb the power of the public sector unions. But it may also be the case that competitive tendering is a step in the direction of true privatisation. Once services are provided by contractors and are bought and sold, then it is a relatively small step to move to private purchasing, whether individually or collectively through insurance schemes. These ideas are advocated by Nicholas Ridley in his pamphlet 'The Local Right' (1988), in which he advocates local authorities being 'enablers, not providers', following the views of those such as Christopher Chope that the public sector should get out of direct service provision wherever possible. Publicly funded provision could be topped up through private means and insurance. The regulations on the implementation of the Community Care legislation in April 1993 specifically say that old people may 'top up' their state benefits to enable them to live in a more expensive establishment.

If enabling involves brokerage on behalf of clients, but with an element of rationing, then public sector managerial work will be completely different. All supervision of service providers will be done by the companies or voluntary agencies. If there are large numbers of providers working to relatively small contracts, then the task of contractor supervision could be a large one, involving bureaucracies of inspectors and checkers.

However, even if these steps are not followed, the introduction of competition has profound implications for the way in which the public sector is managed. It substitutes contracts with tight specifications of service levels and prices for employment contracts; it structurally reduces the power of trades unions; and it breaks up the large organisatons in which the public sector has been traditionally organised.

NOTES

1. Kieron Walsh and I met an engineer who acted as both client and agent. He frequently wrote memos to himself complaining about the standard of work (see Flynn and Walsh, 1982).
2. For more detail on the trade union response to competitive tendering, see Beaumont (1992).
3. Williamson (1975) defines opportunism as the use of threats which are possible because the seller has more information than the buyer, but which the seller does not intend to put into action.

7

A USER-ORIENTED SERVICE

In the preceding chapter we saw that contractual relationships force organisations to define their services precisely. However, the contracts being established are mainly confined to the organisation and its contractors, rather than involving the users of the services. In this chapter we examine ways of making public services responsive to the people who use them.

There is a fundamental difference between developing a customer orientation in the private sector and a user orientation in public services. Companies' marketing efforts are directed at reaching the right number of right customers to buy their products or services, usually in competition with others. Often in the public sector this is not the case: the problem for the organisation may not be to attract people to the services, but rather to deter too many people from applying for them and to ensure that only those people whose needs are defined by the policy receive them. The first task in making a service more responsive to its users is to clarify the relationships between the organisation and its users, of which the customer relationship is only one.

WHAT SORT OF SERVICE RELATIONSHIP?

In the public sector the service relationship is varied and complex. At one extreme is the prison service. The 'users' are convicted people

145

who are being held captive unwillingly. There is no value in treating them as if they have any choice about whether to use the service. Certainly, if one of the objectives of the prison service is to rehabilitate prisoners so that they commit no more offences, the service can be designed to achieve that end more effectively. But, while the prisoners are the users, is there anyone analogous to the 'customer', such as magistrates and judges? When people are sentenced to prison, the prison service offers to magistrates a set of expectations that it will carry out some retribution and achieve some rehabilitation of the prisoner. In a sense the prison service is in competition with other sentencing options, such as probation or fines, which offer alternative service expectations. Or is the general public the customer, to whom the prison service offers protection? And what of the victims of crime: are they not also in a sense the customers of the service? The managers of the prison service have to consider all of these relationships when they design and present the service.

Or consider the accident and emergency departments of hospitals. Their 'customers' usually have no choice: the emergency services deliver them to the most convenient accident and emergency department for treatment. The service has to be fast and responsive to greatly fluctuating demand. The service design problems here are operational matters concerned with making sure that as much treatment as possible is provided within the available resources. There also have to be clear messages about how the service can be accessed, when it is and is not available, and what it should be used for.

Other services relieve distress but create dependency and possibly stigma for the recipients. Most people dependent on social security benefits have no alternative sources of help. Dependency on the monopoly supplier of help can lead to a loss of self-esteem. Unless the service is intended to create this effect, encouraging people to look elsewhere for help, the design problem is one of creating an atmosphere in which the 'customers' can retain some dignity. Long queues in dirty waiting areas have the opposite effect.

There is another category of service which really has no end user. Advice on policy matters to national and local politicians is an important part of many public sector managers' tasks. The minister or committee are the customers for these activities. They may or may not have alternative sources of advice from their political party and from external experts. The service design problem in these cases is about establishing trust in the expertise and integrity of those providing the advice. Policy advice services need to be politically acceptable and, to a degree, predictable.

Politicians are 'customers' for most public sector managers. Politicians who vote money and exercise political control are important constituents for public services. If the politicians want the service to be run in a way which differs from the managers' professional or managerial judgement, it would be a brave person who ignored them. This may lead managers into a position where they have a split managerial personality, facing the users with one set of behaviours and the politicians with another.

In these examples, the relationship between service providers and service users is different from that between a business and its customers. The first question in service design is therefore: 'For whom is the service designed?' The answer will not always be a single person or group. The prison service is designed to satisfy magistrates and judges, the general public, the prison officers, the prisoners, the government and the civil servants in the Home Office. Not surprisingly, these demands pull in contradictory directions. The same is true of many other services. A genuinely friendly and dignified array of personal social services may attract more service users and thus increase the amount of cash spent. This might be better for the users, and make life more pleasant for the staff, but it would probably result in a breach of the social services department's budget.

So, even the question 'who is the customer?' causes problems. The only solution is to design services in ways which are appropriate for the actual relationship involved: there is no point in designing the social security delivery system, for example, as if the users had a choice: this will only cause a spurious sense of caring, and possibly resentment among the users.[1] In this chapter the word 'user' is adopted, but it is intended to cover all the relationships between the service providers and their clients, customers, consumers, and so on.

Careful service design should be able to overcome the objections to planned service delivery which we encountered in Chapter 4: that there are no adequate signals between users and providers and that those signals are lost in the communication mechanisms; there are no incentives for the services to be efficient or of high quality because there is no competition between providers.

ELEMENTS OF A USER-ORIENTED SERVICE

What do the users think?

The starting point for designing a service for the user rather than for the provider is to find out what the existing and potential users think about the service. Even if people have no choice at all it is worth finding out how they perceive the service and what preferences they have. One example of the difference between the providers' and the users' perceptions of what is important is the attitudes to transportation to daycare facilities in social services. A social services department found that the drivers thought that the service should be provided in ambulances by uniformed drivers. The users of the same service thought that the ambulances implied that the users were ill and dependent and preferred taxis with 'civilian dress' drivers. As it happened, the use of smaller vehicles would also cut down journey times and be cheaper.

A general practitioner recently conducted a survey of users of GP surgeries to ascertain the important features of the service from their point of view and contrasted those results with the priorities implied in the White Paper 'Working for Patients' (HMSO, 1989a). The survey showed that the priorities of patients were completely different from those of the drafters of the White Paper. This should not be surprising since no user survey was conducted prior to the White Paper.

There are various techniques for finding out what users think. The simplest is to listen to the employees who are in contact with them. While these contact, or 'front line', staff will not necessarily give an unbiased view, they certainly know more about the users than the management do. Systematic use of this information requires that the front line staff believe that their views will be taken seriously and that what they learn is valid. What the organisation does with this information is another question. Genuinely responsive services are often best provided when the front line has control of its resources.

There are ways of listening to the users without needing to rely on the front line as intermediaries. Specially convened user groups, sometimes called 'focus' groups, can be useful ways of testing reactions to services or trying out new ideas for services. The BBC asks groups of viewers and listeners to give their reactions to programmes. Health authorities can consult the community in a similar way, although what happens as a result of the consultations is left to the health authorities.

Surveys can also elicit reactions to services. Local authorities, health authorities and central government departments regularly use market research companies to measure user and public satisfaction and to find out how to make the services correspond more closely to people's preferences and perceptions.

Systematic analysis of complaints can be a useful source of information. Most police authorities keep records of complaints, but they only record those complaints which reach the 'official complaint' stage when somebody feels strongly enough to give evidence in an investigation. If they were interested in user satisfaction they would seriously consider any complaint about the way users experience the service. Recent surveys have shown, for example, that satisfaction with the police service actually diminishes as people have more personal contact with it. Health authorities generally take complaints very seriously and investigate each one that arrives in written form. Only by following up individual complaints will the organisation know if there is something wrong. Complaints are an opportunity for improvement.

In the Northamptonshire Police Force each subdivision is required to contact a random selection of people who have had contact with the police to find out what they thought of the service they received. The information which this process produces is then used to try to improve the service.

Existing users are not the only people who must be contacted. Those services which fail to reach their targets need to contact those people who should be using the services but do not. Cervical cancer screening reaches disproportionately to middle-class women. If a wider group of users is to be attracted, then the people who do not use them need to be contacted and asked what deters them.

Core and peripheral services

All services consist of elements which constitute the core and other elements which constitute the peripheral aspects. The core of a retail banking service is running the accounts, accepting deposits, making cash accessible and paying interest. These are core services in the sense that if a bank failed to do them, it would cease to be a bank. However, since all banks might be expected to carry out these services, they are not the items which distinguish one bank from another. From the customers' point of view banks are distinguished by their spread of branches, the length of queues in them, the opening hours, the details of the way accounts are kept and charged for, the civility of the staff and the colour of the cheque books. Hence, any retail bank which puts all its efforts into the core of the business and ignores the peripherals will lose in competition.

Users of public services also see them as a set of core and peripheral services, even when there is no competition, and they see the core as the most important element. In the user survey of general practitioner services referred to above, the quality of the consultation with the doctor was rated the most important item of the service package. Ensuring that the core of the service meets user expectations is obviously a key task. But the peripherals also need attention. If the core of a school's service is teaching the basic curriculum, the success with which it does so is obviously important, but, as far as pupils and parents are concerned, so is the treatment of the peripherals. Surveys of parents have shown that atmosphere and apparent 'discipline' are important items which colour opinions of their children's schools. Peripheral activities, such as music tuition, school plays and trips, are also important. Managers of schools need to ensure the right quality and quantity of the peripheral activities as well as the core if they are to make the service user-oriented. Too often the response to financial stringency is to cut back on activities which are unimportant from the producers' point of view because they are peripheral, but which are important from the users' point of view because they are highly visible.

In the case of services provided by professionals, there may be some elements which need to be under professional control and others which can be left to the users. In hospitals, for example, nursing is something which may be more appropriately kept under professional control, while other aspects of the routine may be more appropriate for user control, such as the interior decor or the aesthetic aspects of the catering. In general, the more peripheral the activity, the more user control there can be over it. Unfortunately, not all professionals see services in that way and wish to maintain control over each aspect of the service, even if the users would feel much better if they controlled it themselves. If services are to be more user-oriented and users are to have more control over them, the peripheral aspects are the obvious place to start.

Customer co-production: creating 'pro-users'

A related question is 'how much work should the customer do?' In almost all services the customer is active. Even in the most opulent restaurants customers have to cut up their own food. The amount of work that customers in restaurants have to do depends on the service design: carrying food to tables, clearing tables, walking to the till to pay the bill are all elements of restaurant service design. How much work the customer is expected to do depends partly on the customers' expectation of the service. Generally, high-priced services imply more service and less work by the customer, but the price paid and the level of service given is often a matter for customer choice.

Public services are often designed without user choice in the amount of effort they contribute towards them. While parents are encouraged to help their children to learn, it is not usual to allow parents' teaching to be a substitute for learning at school. Some parents have much more interest and ability in teaching than others, but this is not taken account of when designing pupils' learning. In some cases parents are invited into the classroom to help, especially in primary schools where they assist pupils' reading, but the choice is made by the school, not by the parents.

In public housing, the main variation in how much the tenant does is in internal decorations. Most authorities offer the option of a rent allowance for painting and decorating as an alternative to the landlord decorating. This option does not normally extend to the outside of the building, usually on the grounds that it is the landlord's responsibility to maintain the fabric. So even if the external woodwork is in bad repair because of shortage of funds, the tenants are still not allowed to repair and maintain it. And this is the case whether the tenant is a person with all the necessary skills or not. The service is designed to be consistent, even if this means that every tenant has the same service, whatever their abilities or preferences.

In leisure facilities, it is often left to sports clubs to organise games, book facilities and collection of fees. This not only allows the sports centre management to get on with other activities, it also develops the clubs. If the sports centre staff take responsibility for all the administration, no responsibility rests on the club members to organise themselves.

If users are very active, they may become as important as the providers of the service. Toffler (1980) states that once the distinction has broken down between producer and consumer, there is a new category, the 'prosumer'.[2] If we are calling the recipient of public services the 'user', we might say that the very active user is a 'pro-user', combining provider and user.

The service boundary between what the user does and what the organisation provides should be defined with the users. In this way, even if the users have no choice of whether or not to accept the service, they have some control over the way in which it is delivered. Once the decision has been made, all the front line staff must be aware of where the boundary is for the different categories of users. Active pro-users can prevent services from becoming bureaucratic and unresponsive.

Timing

Most textbooks on service management make the point that it is not possible to store services. Manufactured goods can be stored when demand is slack and released when it picks up. Production can be steady while demand fluctuates. This model is breaking down somewhat in manufacturing, where more and more production is organised to be 'just in time' or delivered when needed. Services have to be either 'just in time' or the users have to be persuaded to accept them when they are available.

In the United Kingdom, and more so in the rest of Europe, banking hours are very restricted. Banks are open when the management and employees think they should open, rather than when customers want the services. Because this makes the service unsatisfactory, banks have substituted machines for bank tellers, so that the pattern of supply matches the pattern of demand. Increasing competition has led to the extension of opening hours.

Matching the timing of supply to the pattern of demand in public services is patchy. It is still possible to find offices which serve the public closed for lunch, a time when working users might be able to reach the office. It is rare to find flexitime arrangements, under which individuals choose their own combinations of working hours, used to extend the hours for which services are open to the public. In some cases flexitime has a defined 'core time element', normally between 10 a.m. and 4 p.m. This eventually becomes the period during which the office is open to the public.

Leisure centres are often closed during leisure time. Many public swimming pools close at midday on Sundays, having been open during normal working hours all week. Weekend opening of offices is rare: regulatory functions such as planning control and building regulations operate during weekdays only. Routine maintenance by housing departments and the utilities which require access to people's homes are usually available only during normal working hours. There are exceptions, especially in the case of emergency services: hospitals, firefighters and the police provide constant cover.

There are two solutions to the mismatch between the timing of demand and the availability of supply. Either the user can be persuaded to conform to the availability of supply, or the supply pattern can be altered. Public transport offers different fares at different times to encourage people to travel at times which match the capacity of the transport system. Some sophisticated computer departments offer lower internal charging rates if users log on outside the peak hours of 11 a.m. to 4 p.m. But if there are no charges levied on the user, their behaviour can be influenced by emphasising the benefits of using the service at those times which are convenient to the supplier. If this is not possible, then the timing of supply should be changed. One housing authority in Scotland reorganised its repair service to operate from 6 a.m. to 6 p.m. so that access could be gained to people's homes before some of the tenants went to work. This reduced the number of 'abortive calls' and improved tenant satisfaction.

Sometimes the organisation is simply not flexible enough to allow this. A school in Birmingham decided to attract adults to attend classes, joining in with the pupils. However, it was unwilling to make any alteration to the timetable to accommodate them: if a subject was taught through a series of single lessons throughout the week, the adults simply had to turn up at those times.

A mutually beneficial exchange

Clearly, altering the timing of supply involves giving the workforce some incentives, just as users need incentives to alter the pattern of demand. This is important in all aspects of matching the needs and preferences of users with the predilections of the organisation.

It is no good simply exhorting the front line, or first line supervision, to become more flexible and fit in with users' preferences. In all aspects of the service exchange,[3] the experience must be worthwhile to both the user and provider. If a front line worker feels undervalued, that worker will express this to the users, will fail to provide a feeling of confidence or value in the user, and will generally contribute to the failure of the service. The value which the organisation places on its front line staff is not just a question of pay, although that is an important element: being taken seriously, being listened to, having a degree of autonomy, are all important aspects of value. The same is true for the user. If the organisation treats the users as a nuisance, or as an interruption to the smooth functioning of the office, the users will feel devalued and will not appreciate the service. This meeting of user and provider is the most crucial element of service design. It can be facilitated by good behaviour on both sides and politeness, courtesy and listening all help. But good behaviour cannot overcome structural impediments to a mutually beneficial exchange. If the police cannot solve crime in a great majority of cases, the fact that they have learned a routine of 'caring behaviour' towards victims does nothing to improve user satisfaction.[4]

The right sort of staff

For all personal services, the rapport between the users and the service providers is important. An important aspect of this is employing the right sort of people. In many cases the first point of contact between the user and the organisation is the reception function, whether this involves a telephone conversation or a face-to-face contact. Reception is a skill which can be learned, but in the public sector it is frequently treated as if it were an unskilled job which can either be done by newly appointed trainees or by people with different skills taking turns on the front desk.

In one district council in Wales, all enquiries for housing repairs, whether telephone or personal callers, are handled by young women who are trainee clerical officers. They have to operate the on-line job control system, classify the repair into categories or urgency, handle complaints from dissatisfied tenants, and are responsible for all queries or requests entering the whole repair system. Fortunately, they are committed and competent, but the question must be asked whether they are the right sort of people for that job.

In some cases, for example in social security, new recruits are given jobs which put them in direct contact with the service users.

When they have gained experience in this position and have undergone training they are often promoted away from such positions. This way of treating the interface with the users guarantees that the service is not as good as it might be. The job of dealing with the users should be treated as the most important one in all service organisations. If this contact is stressful, management needs to ensure that the workers, who might be described as 'emotional labourers', are given sufficient breaks from their job and that they generally receive psychological support.

A second important aspect of the fit between the people at the front line and the user is the matching of age, race and gender. While it is not always possible to have services provided by people who match the client, a permanent mismatch will cause disenchantment with the service. If all teachers are white in areas where the school population is predominantly black, or if all doctors available to treat women are men, there are likely to be breakdowns in the nuances of meaning, in the values shared by the users and providers, and in the relevance of the services. In the case of social services it is rare for social workers to come from 'problem' families. One of the reasons for the growth in voluntary provision of services by organisations among black people is that the predominantly white culture of the public provision is irrelevant for that section of the users. 'Equal opportunities' policies are relevant for the job prospects of those who are otherwise likely to be discriminated against. They are also relevant in matching the service to its users.

Physical aspects

So far, we have considered relatively intangible aspects of service design. Services revolve around the interface between the front line and the user. However, in all services there are physical aspects, whether these are pieces of paper, buildings, vehicles, machinery or furniture. Inappropriate physical surroundings or technology can lead to breakdown in the service.

Public services are often delivered in buildings that have been inherited from other uses. There are geriatric hospitals which used to be workhouses, primary schools which still have 'boys' and 'girls' carved in stone over different entrances, benefit offices designed in the days when there were few claimants, old people's homes built when it was acceptable for an old person to share a bedroom with five others. Very often the people who work in these surroundings get used to them and after a few years, or even months, of working there fail to 'see' the surroundings at all, and certainly fail to see them from the users' point of view. Sometimes this has disastrous results. Potential users fail even to approach the organisation because of the building, because it is intimidating, because it is impossible to find the right office, or because the impression created by the building is at odds with the quality of service available. This has become increasingly difficult as budgets have been squeezed: decoration, signposts, reception areas are seen as peripheral to the main purpose of the organisation and are the first to suffer from cuts. In schools which are managing their own budgets, one of the items on which savings can be made is fuel. This often means that the entrance hall to the school is unlit and unheated. The first point of contact for parents, potential pupils, not to mention existing pupils and staff, is gloomy and unwelcoming.

In one historic city in the north of England, many of the local authority offices are in listed buildings. Because of this there is a restriction on the number and size of notices which can be put up, with the result that the buildings look beautiful but the users cannot find out where to go. In an opposite case, a social services department discovered from its users that they felt discouraged from contacting the department because there was simply a door in a corridor, with no indication of what lay behind it. Once the wall was demolished and an open reception area installed, the intimidation was reduced.

Forms and letters are another important physical aspect of services. Plain English is not yet universally accepted as the way to write to English-speaking users, nor do all organisations ensure that their material is available in all the languages which their users speak. This is because forms and letters are often written from the writer's point of view rather than the reader's. If writers know the meaning of jargon words or technical terms, then they assume that this language will be adequate for the reader. The physical quality of letters and forms is also important. Photocopying breaks down on the third or fourth generation of copying. This is well known to people who use photocopiers, but there is often a feeling that 'it will do; after all it's only the last hundred copies'. For the person reading the copied material, it is not the last hundred, it is the only one. An illegible letter is worse than no letter at all. It signals an attitude which regards the recipient as less important than the sender.

Many services rely on vehicles. The fire brigades understand the messages which shiny red fire appliances signal to their workforce and the public. The vehicles are cleaned every time they leave the fire station whether they need it or not. The users like to see shiny red engines and to know they will turn up in case of emergency. But what messages are sent by the other vehicles used by public services such as buses with opaque, dirty windows or meals on wheels vans which look as if they are in need of care and attention themselves?

Packaging

These physical aspects of services are important in their own right, but they are also an aspect of the way in which the service is packaged or presented. Packaging for physical products is an art-form, and packaging for services is even more difficult because it consists of both physical and intangible aspects of the service.

A service cannot be packaged until the service provider can produce a succinct statement of what the service does, as seen from the user's point of view. Take a museum: the statement of what it does could range from 'this is a convenient place to shelter from the rain' to 'this is an educational establishment where I can learn all about the history of this city' or 'an ace caff with a museum attached', which was an advertising agency's interpretation of the users' view of the Victoria and Albert museum in London.

Packaging is not only important where people have a choice of whether to use the service or not. It is part of the process of creating a shared understanding among staff and between staff and users about what the service does and does not do. Croydon Education Authority (among others) produces a brochure for each of its primary school pupils which sets out what happens in the schools and details what pupils can be expected to do as a result of the various educational experiences they will go through. The brochure is a description of two elements of the service package: the features of the educational process and the benefits which the pupil can expect to derive from it.

Once the service package has been agreed, it needs to be presented to the users and potential users. The physical aspects of the service need to be integrated into a consistent approach to communications. The messages which the organisation wishes to transmit should be sent consistently through all the communication channels to all the audiences. Sometimes the images are not consistent. Take the computer department which designs a new logo, packages its services in a comprehensible set of offerings and does nothing to change the elitist, inward-looking and scruffy staff. All its efforts in image management to improve its relations with its internal users will fail at the point of service delivery.

Or consider the hospital which puts all its user-contact staff through a customer care programme, as a result of which all patients are greeted by name, all staff wear name badges and reception areas are redesigned with the patients' preferences in mind. But the appointments system is still designed with the consultants' wishes to have permanent queues outside their rooms. Inconsistent messages are transmitted. Reception staff are sending the message 'we care about you and value you and your time', while the doctors are saying 'our time is more valuable than yours'.

Consider the messages transmitted by the social security system. One message is 'every claimant is a potential fraud and the system must be designed to stop you getting away with any penny to which you are not entitled'. This is reinforced when ministers pursue popularity at party conferences by declaring war on 'scroungers'. Another says: 'not enough people who are entitled to benefit are claiming it; please come along to the office and make a claim.' Unfortunately for the front line staff, both of these messages are expected to be transmitted at the same time. It would be relatively easy to transmit either message consistently, through all the communication channels. The latter message would be transmitted through advertising campaigns targeted at non-users, friendly treatment at benefit offices, opening hours which are convenient to users, easily understood literature and simple forms.

Apart from the problems posed by inconsistent messages, the other complication in managing an image for public sector organisations is that managers may wish to transmit different messages to different audiences. They may wish to demonstrate to their controlling politicians that they are efficient, brisk and ruthless, while presenting an image of friendliness to potential users. This is all part of the dilemma we discussed earlier: who is the 'customer' of the service? If the 'customer' is the minister, then the message may be one set of images; if the 'customer' is the user, another set is required. In some cases there is no compromise and the organisation and its managers have to live facing both ways.

Because of this, many managers in the public sector are frustrated by exhortations about values from management gurus from the private sector. They would love to be able to manage within a single set of shared values and run their organisations so that those values are expressed through all the organisations' actions. The reality is that there are many values competing simultaneously.[5] Establishing a 'culture' or a set of values which permeates the whole organisation is not a simple matter.

CULTURE AND VALUES

Discussion of the management of organisational culture as part of the management task slips in and out of fashion in management literature. Pascale and Athos (1982) emphasise the importance of the management of 'superordinate goals', defined as 'the significant meanings or guiding concepts that an organisation imbues in its members' (p. 81). They believe that these goals 'tie the purposes of the firm (e.g. goods, services, profits) to human values. We believe that this linkage to human values is growing in importance' (p. 187). The Audit Commission also put the management of values at the centre of the management process.[6] Richard Normann (1991) puts 'Culture and Philosophy' at the centre of his approach to service management, as the unifying force in service organisations. While values of people inside the organisation are derived partly from society in general, they can also be influenced by the leadership within. Peters and Waterman (1982) included 'hands-on value driven' management as one of their prescriptions for good management, believing that successful organisations develop a culture where values are shared.

In the current climate in the public sector there are three fundamental questions. Is it possible to create organisations in which everybody shares the same values? Is it necessary for responsive service delivery that all employees share the same values? Is it possible to influence people's behaviour by creating structures in which they can work well, even though the underlying values are not shared?

People have various motivations for the jobs they do. Even in the current climate it is unlikely that many people are attracted to public sector jobs because they believe these offer the highest available rewards, except in areas of the country where alternative job opportunities are scarce. Hence, they are likely to be motivated by other factors, such as job security and/or a desire to work in an environment where profit is not the primary motive either for themselves or the organisation. Or they may feel that what they are doing is 'just a job' to which they have no special commitment. It is very likely that there will be conflicting values which cannot be resolved. For example, the organisation may have a primary value of either profit or service (and these could lead to different practices) and individuals could be motivated primarily by money or by other things, once their basic income is secured. If we plot these two possibilities, we can see the possible combinations of individual and organisational values (see Figure 7.1). If the organisation is mainly concerned with profits and the staff are motivated by money, it is relatively easy to design incentive and reward systems which all go in the same direction (quadrant 1). Even then, if parts of the organisation require creativity, for example, and people are motivated by the opportunity to be creative, cash rewards may not be the most appropriate mechanism of incentive or reward.

But if the organisation is interested in financial targets and the people are motivated by a public service ethos (quadrant 3), the incentive systems have to be designed so that rewards go to those whose behaviour promotes the targets. For example, a local authority housing department may be staffed by people who are mainly interested in providing a helpful service to tenants. If housing management offices are established as profit centres and are given targets relating mainly to rent arrears, rather than providing help for tenants in difficulties, there will be tension between front line staff and senior management. This situation is already arising in those local authorities where priorities have shifted as a result of balancing the housing revenue accounts.

Quadrant 3 should present fewer problems, since the basic values are shared, but in quadrant 4 where individuals are motivated by money, while the organisation is interested in service, the incentive systems have to be designed so that behaviour conducive to the organisation's motivations is rewarded. Performance-related pay, for example, would have to be related to standards of behaviour rather than financial targets.

The introduction of performance-related pay assumes that people will perform 'better' if there is a financial incentive. Organisations

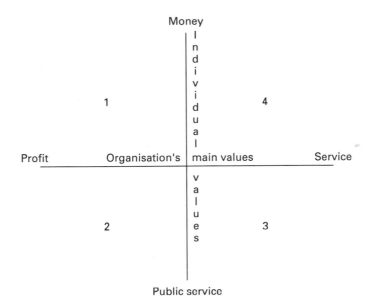

Figure 7.1 Individual and organisational values

which introduce this wish to move from quadrant 3 to either 4 or 1. In some cases managers who receive performance-related pay are actually demotivated, expressing the view that they were previously working as hard and effectively as they could and that additional payments can make no difference. This is especially so when only a few people are rewarded for the results of a team effort. In one Inland Revenue office the manager spends his performance bonus on the staff, in recognition of the team's contribution.

There are other possible positions which are not given on the diagram: what if the staff are not particularly motivated at all, either by money or public service? They just turn up for work and put in the minimum effort required. In this case, financial or other incentives will not necessarily improve performance.

Shared values as a management tool will work only if it is possible to create a congruence between what drives individuals and what the organisation wishes to achieve. If the values are not shared, management's task is to ensure that the incentives, rewards and controls encourage behaviours which correspond to the organisation's values.

CONCLUSION

Managing services requires a different approach from managing manufacturing, mainly because the service organisation continuously has to recreate the relationship between itself and its users. The relationship has to be defined within the users' perception of the service. Then the whole organisation has to focus its efforts on ensuring the service encounter occurs according to the design.

Managing public services is different from managing private ones. While there is a wide variety of private services, the objective is always the same: to create a service which is sufficiently valuable to the customers to persuade them to buy it. In the public sector, the objective is not always to generate revenues, and in many cases the users are forced to co-operate and have no choices. This means that each type of relationship between the organisation and its users needs to be reflected in the actions of its staff.

Unfortunately, there is no slick solution. Each organisation needs to understand its environment, its task, its workforce and its relationship with its users.

If the beliefs and values of all employees are consistent with their actions, then this is a bonus and makes management easier, but 'value management' is not a substitute for good service design or for an organisation which has clear accountabilities and responsibilities and which supports and reinforces appropriate behaviour.

NOTES

1. 'Customer care' training in which front line staff are drilled in smiling and saying 'have a nice day' can have this effect.
2. Toffler (1987, pp. 275–6) cites the example of the do-it-yourself pregnancy testing kit which allows women to side-step the doctor and provide a service for themselves.
3. What Richard Normann (1990) calls 'the moment of truth'.
4. I was once the victim of a series of burglaries. After the second in rapid succession I was telephoned by the desk sergeant to be told: 'We are still working on it.' I asked which burglary they were working on and he said: 'I don't know, I'm just getting through the paperwork.' The sergeant was now honestly expressing the truth that the police do not solve burglaries but try to maintain public support by learning 'customer care' routines.
5. Quinn (1988) says that all management is a matter of coping with

competing values. Hampden-Turner (1990) analyses how managers can manage dilemmas.
6. The first two controllers at the Audit Commission were ex-McKinsey consultants, like Pascale and Athos.

8

ORGANISATIONAL STRUCTURES

There was a time when reorganisation was seen as the automatic solution to problems in the public sector. It was felt that it was sufficient to create new local authorities, each with new management structures, in order to produce better managed local services. Create a new structure of health authorities with hierarchical relationships and the health service will be better managed. During the great reorganisations of the 1970s the view that economies of scale were prevalent dominated. The local government reorganisation of 1974 (1975 in Scotland) created fewer, larger local authorities. The Departments of Trade and Industry and Environment were created through mergers of smaller departments.

There are currently many pressures forcing public sector organisations to restructure in one way or another. In Chapter 6 we have seen that new contractual relationships have been established in health, education, the civil service and those parts of local government which are subject to competitive tendering. In effect, these changes are reorganisations which are at least as significant as those carried out in the 1970s in which new organisations were created.

FRAGMENTATION

The traditional organisations of the welfare state are breaking up. For example, local government is splitting up into more independent units, with schools running themselves, social services divided into specifiers and providers, housing departments splitting up and being disbanded. When combined with privatisation and contracting-out, this leads even more to the development of networks of suppliers, with centrally controlled funding, rather than to the traditional organisational bureaucracies. It is unlikely that these tendencies are reversible. If there has been a change in consensus since the immediate post-war period it is surely that large centralised public bureaucracies are not the ideal organisational form.[1] This tendency has important implications for managers. First, if they run a service delivery unit, they might expect to accept a greater degree of responsibility earlier in their careers. The experience of decentralisation in social services departments has been that team and area managers are quite capable of taking on budgeting, financial management and resource control. If the units of management are to be smaller and under more local control, many more people will need to be willing and able to take up managerial positions.

This may also imply that more people make a whole career running units, rather than expecting to move up the hierarchy. If the real managerial jobs are being performed at unit level (hospital, school, police station), it would be inappropriate to move the best managers out of those positions and into a headquarters function. It is already the case in those organisations which have decentralised that the jobs at the 'centre' become less and less interesting once the real power and responsibility is devolved.

The skills required for running decentralised networks are also different from those required in bureaucratic hierarchies. For example, deals need to be struck with other organisations or parts of organisations. These must be of mutual benefit if they are to work, and thus need to be negotiated in that light. This process is different from that of persuading a subordinate or a superior from a clear, unequal power position. Negotiating skills become as important as persuasion and leadership.

The content of managerial jobs in independent units is also different because there is less scope for specialisation of managerial tasks when there are fewer managers per unit. This implies a demand for general management at unit level.

There are also implications for the organisations as entities. The focus of organisational design should be the service delivery unit whose manager should be given a clear set of limits of authority and accountability. This should not only concern money and other resources, but also the standards of service which are expected. These standards must be defined and agreed in conjunction with the unit manager. If there is a contract for the service, this can become a useful focus for the definition of service standards. If innovation is expected, this must also be made clear.

Second, the whole of the rest of the organisation exists to help the service delivery unit do its job, or to keep it under control. If the unit manager has a clearly specified remit and is genuinely accountable, most control should result automatically from the accountability mechanism. This implies that HQ functions, such as personnel and finance, should be mainly supporting, rather than controlling, functions. It also implies that middle managers are enablers and supporters rather than supervisors and message carriers.[2] There is, however, a continuing 'audit' role. Politicians at both central and local government levels need mechanisms to monitor the implementation of their policies. This is likely to be an HQ function.

Genuine decentralisation of decision-making and control requires two things of the top managers. They have to ensure that the support mechanisms are relevant to the managers' jobs; and they may have to relinquish control of the support services to the front line managers. For example, the managers themselves should be able to specify the management information which they require. If those responsible for producing it are unable to do so properly, the managers themselves should be allowed to produce their own. The same is true of the rest of the support services.

MACHINES, BRAINS AND POLITICS

It is very difficult for bureaucracies to adjust to a new focus of management effort on the service delivery unit. Some changes which might appear trivial to an outsider are important for the organisations. For example, in a videotape which was made to promote the establishment of executive agencies there is an interview with the manager of a large office in Companies House. She is delighted that since the change to agency status she can now buy her own envelopes when the office runs out of them. This change is presented as a major advance.

The problem is one of changing the way people think about their position in the organisation. If somebody has spent an entire career receiving instructions and carrying them out, it is difficult for them to take the initiative, especially when a failure is given more importance than a success. Similarly, people who have had authority over money or personnel procedures find it uncomfortable to give up that authority and let it shift to the manager of a service delivery unit.

In the period when public sector organisations were being designed from scratch (during the great reorganisations) the dominant metaphor was that of the organisation as a machine, with hierarchical systems of planning and control based on the notion of a single 'rationality' which could be imposed on the organisation from the top, whether from general managers or chief executives.[3] Single chains of command were established, with clear accountabilities and lines of communication which could be represented on the organisation charts. Indeed, in some cases the charts came first. Many local authorities copied the structures suggested in the Bains Report without further thought.[4]

There was some variation in this way of thinking, with some people arguing that public sector organisations should be more like brains and should be developed so that they could learn to capture and process information and thus be more responsive to their environments. These 'brains' might prove to be more messy structures than the machines because learning and information processing does not only occur at the top of the organisation. Simple hierarchical structures are less useful for learning than for control. However, the general pattern was to attach a research and intelligence unit to the machine. This could have as much or as little impact as the machine wished.

Yet others have seen the public sector organisations as political systems and that the only way of making sense of them is to analyse the power relationships within them, i.e. to interpret the activities of managers and workers as attempts to gain power. If this means that they have to make alliances with the users, or with other elements outside the organisation, they may do so, but only in pursuit of their own power. This literature includes such writers as Peter Jackson (1982), who argues that people working in public sector organisations, like everyone else, try to maximise their own income and satisfaction.

When we consider organisations in the public sector, we have to be clear about the models or metaphors we are using. They not only colour our thinking, they also make managers follow particular actions. There are often conflicting models in existence. Some of the caring professions think of the organisation as a family or an organism while the managers see it as a machine. When the managers use language and behaviour appropriate to a machine the workers may take no notice.

CENTRALISATION AND DECENTRALISATION

Even if we move away from the machine metaphor and focus the organisation on service delivery, there are still important questions about how much decentralisation there should be. In none of the reforms is there a suggestion that units become completely autonomous, like corner shops, for example. Schools are still attached to education authorities or directly to the Department for Education or one of its quangos. Hospital trusts are not completely independent of the NHS.

Part of the unease with the monolithic bureaucracies was that the service delivery units had too little autonomy. Management by rigid rules made them unable to respond to their users. As a consequence of this thinking, various attempts have been made to reorganise through decentralisation. The Royal Mail has decentralised its operation to give more authority and responsibility to its district managers. Many housing authorities have physically pushed the housing management function into the housing estates. In some cases combinations of local authority services have been decentralised to neighbourhood level, notably in Walsall, Islington and Tower Hamlets. In many social services departments, decentralisation has taken the form of teams and areas being given more control over their resources.[5] Physical dispersal of staff and services is not necessarily accompanied by a managerial decentralisation of control over the services.

Decentralisation may be a passing fashion. In some cases the decentralisation has been pushed through by politicians acting out of conviction. It may not be the best answer to all organisational problems, any more than centralised hierarchies were. What are the factors which determine how much decentralisation there should be?

One criterion is the degree of complexity in the environment. Henry Mintzberg (1983) suggests that if the environment is very complex, it is more effective to have decentralised organisation in order to make sense of the complexity. However, Mintzberg also suggests that if the environment is hostile and difficult, the organisation should have centralised decision-making in order to be able to protect itself from that environment. He suggests that the reaction to a hostile environment, even one of great complexity, should be to centralise, if only temporarily (p. 142).

The elements of threat in the public sector organisation's environment are threats to the budget from the budget provider(s), and competitive threats from others who are able to provide the service. In Chapter 6 we saw that the introduction of competition can create a threatening environment. If the only response to this is some radical changes in the organisation, they will be carried out more quickly and effectively if they are centrally controlled.

The other element which Mintzberg believes affects the degree of standardisation and formalisation of work and its supervision, and therefore its centralisation, is the degree of dynamism in the environment. He suggests that if the environment is changing quickly, standardisation is inappropriate and people have to be given freedom to operate in relatively non-standard ways (p. 138). But if the environment is complex, changing and threatening, we have contradictory approaches: intelligence-gathering needs to be decentralised, standardised procedures do not work, but decision-making needs to be centralised to respond to threats.

One response in the private sector is to establish centralised, tight financial control over operating units, but to allow them operational freedom. Units have set financial targets, have to justify capital expenditure through an analysis of the returns on investment, but are allowed to run the business themselves. In the public sector it is not so easy to do this, not least because financial returns are frequently not the main criterion of success. Tight financial control only gives control over expenditure and not over all the other elements. In the public services there are three additional elements which influence the degree of centralisation.

First, if the work done is very complicated and not susceptible to detailed scrutiny, then it is not possible to have a centralised control mechanism for the work process. If it is also difficult to measure or evaluate the outputs or outcomes (see Chapter 5), then it is impossible to organise for tight central control. If central control is required for some reason, such as the Secretary of State for Education's distrust of teachers, then either scrutiny of the process or measurement of the outcome must be established. The only alternative is decentralisation, in the sense of leaving the operatives, in this case the teachers, alone to determine their own actions. If outcomes can be measured, then the practitioners can more effectively demand to be left alone to manage the service processes. Accountability can focus on outcomes and effectiveness rather than on resource use.

The second element is whether there is agreement about the most effective ways of running the service. If all probation officers, for example, agreed about which programmes were most likely to produce desirable results for offenders, then there would be no need for central scrutiny of their activities and they could be a self-regulated profession. Because there is uncertainty about the relationship between process and outcomes, central scrutiny takes place.

Third, what is the degree of risk involved if a decentralised service breaks down? The fire service has very hierarchical centralised structures, which are based on the command methods used on the firegrounds. If, while a fire is burning, firefighters engage in debates and disagreements about the best way to organise the squirting of the water, the resultant risks become very high. Similarly, if loose procedures in recording potential dangers to children result in visits by social workers being missed, children's lives may be in danger. In these circumstances tight control over procedures is essential. However, the people at the centre of highly centralised organisations can also make disastrous mistakes.

The above three elements are combined with Mintzberg's three criteria in Table 8.1. Different combinations pull in different directions. In reality, certain aspects are decentralised while others are centralised. Even in decentralised local authorities, such as the London Borough of Tower Hamlets, crucial decisions on resource allocation are still arrived at centrally. We need to be very clear about exactly what is being decentralised.

So far we have only considered the location of the authority over operational matters and finance. We can break these decisions down further into questions of what sort of service to provide, for which

Table 8.1 Determinants of centralisation

Complexity of environment	High	→	Decentralisation
	Low	→	Centralisation
External threats	High	→	Centralisation
	Low	→	Decentralisation
Need for innovation and non-standard work because of changing environment	High	→	Decentralisation
	Low	→	Centralisation
Complex, difficult to define task	High	→	Decentralisation
	Low	→	Centralisation
Consensus on best approach	High	→	Decentralisation
	Low	→	Centralisation
Risk associated with failure	High	→	Centralisation
	Low	→	Decentralisation

users, in what quantity and with what degree of discretion over resource use.

What to produce?

In professional service organisations, the detailed answer to the question 'what to produce?' is often a matter of professional judgement. A doctor, for example, does not expect to receive instructions from a supervisor about what to do for a patient whose condition the doctor has just diagnosed. Teachers feel that they know best what is good for their pupils. In public organisations, politicians have an important role in deciding what services should be provided, although this is usually expressed in general terms.

A traditional way of making decisions has been to establish a hierarchy of general aims which are refined into objectives and targets, corresponding to levels in the organisational hierarchy. These decisions are then executed through 'management by objectives' (MBO), a system of top-down management control. This is one aspect of the approach to organisations which views them as machines. It is worth noting that, by 1955, Drucker had already suggested that MBO should be a process in which managers agreed their objectives and targets with their superiors, on the grounds that each functional manager was better able to judge what was desirable and necessary for the organisation than his or her supervisor.[6]

Decisions on what to produce are in reality a result of such a process of discussion and negotiation. Whoever is held ultimately accountable will have the last word in the discussions.

For whom?

The second important organisational design question is 'who decides who receives the service?' There are two extreme answers: at one extreme the users themselves decide whether to receive the service and from where; at the other end there could be a centrally planned allocation mechanism which establishes rules for entitlement, and those rules are carried out mechanically lower down the organisation. In between these extremes are various degrees of delegation of decision-making to the various parts of the organisation. For example, a school could decide on its own level of admissions and on the selection of pupils; or it could simply provide the service for all those pupils allocated to it by the local education authority.

How much?

The volume of service, reflected in the budget, can also be decided at different levels. In a market system the volume is determined by demand. If units of a business generate more sales, they grow, subject to investment being approved by head office. In a non-market system this is not possible because the extra sales do not generate extra revenue. The volume of service provided is determined by some form of budget process. It is difficult to imagine the overall budget for a government department, local authority or health authority being determined at the level of the service delivery units unless a market is operating or the service is purely demand-led, such as the demand for driving tests.

How much discretion?

The degree to which the budget for a unit in the organisation is broken down into specific activities is also important. The extremes for a unit might be: 'here is a budget of £x million, spend it how you wish' and 'here is your budget broken down into the precise amounts which you are expected to spend on each activity'. The private sector solution of tight financial control and loose operational control can be translated into 'one-line budgets'. These are allocated to service delivery units, which then have complete discretion over how to deploy them, subject to policy and service delivery targets.

In the public sector there are usually adverse consequences for the organisation that overspends budgets. Any management structure that allows budgets to get out of control is therefore suspect. This does not mean that financial control cannot be delegated to a low level, rather that the procedures for financial control must work. It is an apparent paradox that the introduction of decentralised management is normally accompanied by very strict financial control. In the case of the decentralisation of management in East Sussex Social Services, for example, an important prerequisite of decentralisation was a guarantee that overall budgetary performance (out-turn within 1.5 per cent of budget) would be maintained.

Each of the four aspects (what to produce, for whom, in what quantity and with what discretion) could be handled with varying degrees of centralisation or decentralisation. If we plot these four dimensions according to the degree to which they are centralised or decentralised, we could draw a profile for different organisations. Consider the education service. Currently, the volume of activity is decided centrally, by the Department for Education and the Department of Environment, as part of the public expenditure decision-making process. Choice of pupils for schools is relatively decentralised. There is some degree of autonomy for schools about the nature of what is taught outside the national curriculum. School budgets offer a large degree of freedom over the deployment of resources. Education authority might have the profile represented by the Xs on Figure 8.1.

At the moment most police forces are organised so that each of the elements is highly centralised, while some are trying to move towards decentralisation of service design, with more autonomy for local divisions. However, budgets (decisions on volume) continue to be made centrally. Since the volume of service to be provided and the criteria for allocation are politically important, it is unlikely that they will ever be fully delegated to front line management, although superintendents have some discretion to decide on the deployment of resources.

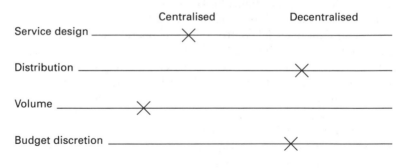

Figure 8.1 The education service

THE LEARNING ORGANISATION

So far we have considered centralisation and decentralisation only with regard to decisions. But if we think of the organisation as also having a learning function (the 'brain' metaphor), we can also see that learning could be centralised or decentralised. An organisation which finds out about its users by setting up a centralised research function is a centralised 'brain'. One which sets up procedures whereby the front line and first line supervision are used as information-gatherers decentralises the intelligence function. It is possible to do this while still centralising decision-making.

If we put the two functions – information-gathering and decision-making – together, we can see that there are various combinations of centralisation and decentralisation, as shown in Figure 8.2. In quadrant 1, where decisions are centralised but learning is decentralised, we have the organisation which practises consultation with its workforce, but does not allow the workforce to make decisions. In important matters (such as budgets and service design) it is still a centralised bureaucracy, although it allows its members some say about what the users think. In quadrant 2, where both decision-making and control are decentralised, the organisation has become an organism which responds by letting those parts which are in touch with the environment respond to it through individual decisions. A loosely run charity might be structured in this way: autonomous local groups are responsible for fund-raising and also make decisions about how the funds raised should be used.

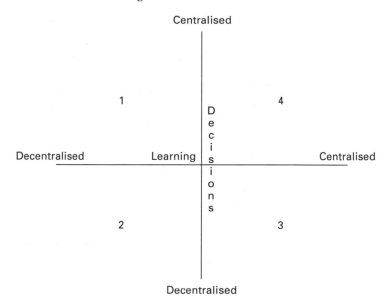

Figure 8.2 Learning and deciding

Quadrant 3, in which there is centralised intelligence and decentralised control is in danger of wasting its time on information-gathering. If the local units are autonomous, they may choose whether or not to listen to the central intelligence-gathering function. Local authorities which have central intelligence units discover that the units spend time and money gathering information which the individual departments may (and frequently do) choose to ignore.

Quadrant 4, in which there is centralised learning and decision-making, is the classic machine bureaucracy where the bosses decide what should be done on the basis of their own information-gathering and interpretation. It is very difficult to establish such systems in professional environments. Professionals will often use their autonomy to ignore the guidance which results from the information-gathering.

Some of the recent reforms in the UK public sector are designed to move organisations from one quadrant to another. The Education Reform Act produced an education system where there are central decisions about what to produce (the curriculum) and how much to spend on it (the education budgets) because it has been decided that the government knows better than local education authorities what the users prefer. The reforms move education (nationally) from quadrant 2 to quadrant 4. At the local level, they move some operational decisions (details on budget use) from the local education authority to the schools.

The reform of the NHS decentralises information-gathering to the market mechanism established between purchasers and service providers. In planning the level of provision, projections can be based on the trends established by thousands of individual choices. In this case the decision-making functions, especially in relation to overall budget, will remain centralised in the Department of Health, while the intelligence-gathering function is decentralised. The NHS is moving from quadrant 4 to quadrant 1. These two changes are plotted in Figure 8.3.

POLITICS

The reasons for these and other reforms are mainly political. In public services official and unofficial politics obviously play a large part. The Conservative government decided that employers' interests were not being adequately served by the education service. Local

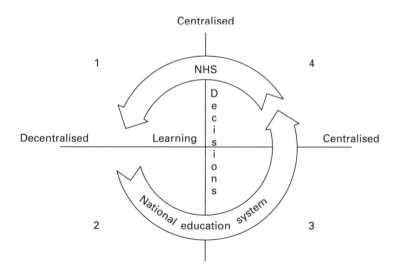

Figure 8.3 Education and health reforms

education authorities were relatively autonomous bodies which were susceptible to control by different interests through the local electoral process. The only solution was to impose a central direction with control and monitoring mechanisms. However, if we refer back to Figure 8.1, we see that there are good reasons to suspect that the attempted centralisation is inappropriate and may fail.

The education process is relatively complex and difficult to monitor, the environment is complex and changing and there is a need for innovation and experiment. These factors point to the need for a decentralised service. The only one which suggests the need for centralisation is the lack of consensus on the best approach to education. The Education Reform Act's solution was to impose an artificial agreement, through the national curriculum.

In the case of the NHS the government believed that it was being blamed for increasing waiting lists, while not being able to achieve its expenditure ambitions. There was frustration at what the government felt was the doctors' unjustified influence on the service.

At lower levels, organisational politics plays a very large part in structural change. At a trivial level, decisions on structure are made to accommodate individuals, thus posts will be created for them. More seriously, the actual relationships which emerge are determined through a political process of bargaining and the exercise of power and influence. Formal changes, such as the introduction of a decentralised structure, can be undermined by such realities. If Head Office staff can, they will resist the transfer of power to lower echelons. The converse is also true, as front line managers find ways to evade central control. These conflicts can direct attention away from the task of service delivery.

MATRIX STRUCTURES

One solution to the problem of organisational design is the matrix structure in which a unit is accountable in two directions. For example, part of a company may be accountable to a regional manager as well as to a product manager.[7] Variants on matrix structure occur in many parts of the public sector. For example, many social services departments have both managers of geographical areas and managers for particular client groups. An individual social worker is accountable, in principle, to both managers for the care offered to a particular client. Medical teams can be accountable both to the head of a speciality and the head of the unit.

The difficulty with matrix structures is that they are unstable. The political process within the organisation is likely to make one line of accountability dominant. Hence, the head of a speciality may have more power than the head of the unit. In recognition of this, some organisations place the emphasis of one line of accountability on the support function and the other on control. For example, in education authorities there are specialist advisers whose job is to maintain and improve the standard of teaching of particular subjects. Heads of departments in schools are accountable to the headteachers but are supported by the specialist advisers.

BIG DECISIONS

There are also important questions of structure outside the individual organisations. The big national decisions about budget allocations are made through a very centralised decision-making process called the public expenditure survey process.[8] Here the large blocks of expenditure are allocated to programmes. Government departments, local authorities and health authorities, and many other organisations, have varying degrees of discretion about how to spend those resources and, in some cases, whether to accept the figures. For example, the government's assessment of each local authority's spending requirement is calculated by adding up a standard level of expenditure for each service. Whether the authorities actually divide up their budgets in this way is up to them. We have seen that the local authorities have had their discretion eroded.

Such a heavily centralised process makes public spending relatively insensitive. For example, expenditure on services for elderly people is spread across many budget headings, including local authority social services spending, health spending and the social security system. The Community Care reform is an attempt to define an overall strategy for spending on caring for elderly people.

This means that strategies have to be decided at operational level. Individual managers in social services and the NHS have to reach agreement on particular schemes. The Audit Commission (1986) has shown that this has not been spectacularly successful. The same is true in other areas in which co-operation is made necessary by structural arrangements. For example, the prison service, the police and the probation service operate in separate organisations. Apart from a policy section in the Home Office, there is no forum where professionals and managers can develop and execute a strategy for the punishment, care and resettlement of convicted people. No single decision is ever made which includes the relative costs and benefits of additions to the prison service and the probation service. The budgets are considered in isolation, as are the strategies.

The problem becomes even more complex when tradeoffs have to be made between different services and different client groups. How are resources to be allocated among old people, schoolchildren, road users and convicted prisoners? At the moment the decisions are made in an extremely aggregated way in the annual public expenditure round. At local authority level, allocation decisions can be made among those services which are under local authority control. Local changes in demography, for example, can be taken account of in resource allocation.

The fundamental structural question is whether the public expenditure survey process can possibly be sufficiently sensitive to allocate expenditure to achieve maximum effect, especially when the level of aggregation is such that individual services can hardly be taken into account. If it cannot, there needs to be a more disaggregated decision-making process in which individual services are identifiable, so that decisions are made about services and not just about sums of money. To be effective, such a process must encompass a range of services since people taking decisions about individual services will naturally defend their own rather than make tradeoffs. These considerations lead to the idea of a local level of government making decisions about the public services in local areas.

CONCLUSION

The public sector has learned from the experience of the great reorganisations. Traditional, hierarchical bureaucracies are only appropriate in a limited set of circumstances. Very rigid controls over budgets and behaviour make service delivery units insensitive to the needs and wishes of their users. If services are to be oriented towards their users, the organisational structure should be designed to ensure that the service delivery unit has sufficient support to be able to do its job. Control over the units is necessary only to ensure that overall budgets are not exceeded and that policy is being followed.

Organisations must recognise the difference between control and support functions. Too often they are mixed up. Accountants are used both to control expenditure and to provide management information. Personnel managers both control recruitment and help with training and selection. Senior managers both control budgets and provide professional support.

There is also a need for clarity about the difference between finding out about the service users and deciding what services to provide. Mechanisms need to be designed to carry out both tasks, and managers of service delivery units have to be clear about the limits of their discretion in both respects.

There are no universal rules about the correct degree of centralisation or decentralisation. However, in all environments, whether hostile or friendly, turbulent or stable, complex or simple, managers of service delivery units can only do their jobs if the rules are clear. Internal politics will change the rules over time but if the individuals in the organisation fight for power to the exclusion of the users, the organisation will lose its support.

In the case of local authorities, their corporate identity requires that they are more than a collection of independent services. Complete decentralisation combined with the widespread use of contractors would fragment the organisations to such a degree that they would no longer be identifiable entities. Survival requires a user-oriented structure which maintains a corporate identity. Where organisations have been split into 'purchasers' and 'providers' it is important to decide who is accountable for services and whose task it is to make the decisions we have discussed. The danger is that the split results in nobody being accountable.

NOTES

1. Peters sees the breakdown of the large company as a parallel feature: the fact that the break-up value of companies is often higher than the value of the company as a single entity is taken as an indication that smaller independent units are more effective than large ones (Lecture, 1989).
2. See Peters (1987, ch. 5).
3. Morgan (1986) has shown that people who work in organisations draw on

metaphors to develop their understanding of them. The metaphors which Morgan claims are in common use include: the machine, the brain, culture, political system, psychic prison, instrument of domination.

4. See Bains (1972).
5. See Flynn (1988).
6. See Drucker (1955, ch. 11).
7. See Hunt (1986, pp. 194–9).
8. See Likierman (1988) for a description of the process.

9

THE FUTURE OF PUBLIC SECTOR MANAGEMENT

INTRODUCTION

When the Central Policy Review staff set out radical options for the transformation of the welfare state in 1982 the Cabinet was so nervous that it kept its discussions of the proposals secret. They thought that even talking about widespread privatisation would be politically embarrassing. And yet, by the early 1990s, almost any radical solution seems possible. Privatisation of the hospitals? It would be a small step from NHS Trust status to privatisation. Privatise pensions, other than a residual safety net state pension? This will happen when current plans come to fruition. Contract out the work of the civil service? This has already been put in train. Abandon national pay scales for public employees? 'Flexible pay' has already moved a long way in this direction.

Many of the changes we have discussed are unlikely to be reversed. The 1993–4 public expenditure round had to cope with the consequences of the fiscal deficit which was caused by the high spending and low tax regime in the period leading up to the 1992 general election. The economic crisis of 1991–2 reduced the level of taxes paid, increased the social security bill and seriously reduced the government's scope to spend. It only managed to keep to its spending target by limiting public sector pay settlements to 1½ per cent.[1] Any reforms which cost money are unlikely in the medium-term future. Any reforms which make expenditure easier to control will be retained. Given the demands placed on the social security budget by consistently high unemployment levels and the growth of the population of pension age, the rest of the public services are likely to have to manage with a level of resources close to present values. The only scope for readjustment in the pattern of spending would be to bring the defence budget down, in line with comparable countries.

However, even if the economic situation will preclude any great increase in spending on public services,[2] the pendulum may swing away from the radical right. There is certainly no public support for the privatisation of the NHS, and the government spent a great deal of money on persuading the public that privatisation was the appropriate approach to water supply.

In this chapter we speculate on the future of management in the public sector, given the alternative policy scenarios.

THE DEMOGRAPHIC FUTURE

There has been a certain amount of dismay recently as the demographic truths make their impact on many sectors of the economy. The recession cured the shortage of labour which was developing in the late 1980s, for example the shortage of nurses which is still a problem, especially in the south-east of England.

The universities and colleges have realised that they are increasingly in a buyers' market and have to compete more actively for students, as well as discovering the idea that education should be something which people can and should have access to at different stages in their lives, not just in their youth.

If the recession turns into another boom period and the demand for labour increases, the labour supply may prove to be a constraint on the public sector as well as the rest of the economy. For example, the number of 16–39-year-olds in the United Kingdom is expected to fall from 20.3 million in 1990 to 19.3 million in 2001 and 18 million in 2011. However, labour shortages in the public sector are as likely to be caused by a continuation of the deteriorating relative pay which we saw in Chapter 1 as by an absolute shortage of people.

The health services are feeling the impact of the growth in the elderly population. In general, the dependency ratio (the ratio of the people of working age to the total population) will become less favourable towards the end of the century. Projections show the population aged 80 and over rising from 2.1 million in 1990 to 2.6

million in 2006. The number of people of working age will decline as a proportion of the population as the number of children increases and the number at or above retirement age stays constant. The implications of these trends are, first, that there will be increasing competition for workers, although the strength of competition will depend on which part of the country you happen to be in. Already, the Departments of Health and of Social Security have moved headquarters and other staff from the south-east to areas where there seemed at the time to be less competition for labour. We can expect this trend to continue in other sectors. Parts of the Inland Revenue, Post Office Savings Bank, Vehicle Licensing and other functions are already located outside the south-east, mainly as a result of previous regional development policies.

Second, there will be a disproportionate call on the resources of the NHS. The population's demand for healthcare increases with age, the very oldest people making the greatest demands.

Third, during the 1990s there will be an increasing demand for education for people of school age. In most parts of the country the days of falling school rolls are over.

VALUES AND THE FUTURE

We have seen that there are conflicting values about the public sector. The 'new right' and their followers believe in individualism, private ownership, profit and 'market forces'. There is also a public service ethic which was part of the post-war consensus and emphasises collective responsibility for certain services, equitable treatment of people regardless of their incomes, and includes a belief that it is wrong to make profits from essential services.

The future of the public sector depends to a large degree on the values which become dominant among those who control public services. Whose values predominate depends on who is most powerful. It is possible that future governments may decide that the managerialist and individualistic approach has gone far enough and that other values should be given a chance, especially if there is no more electoral advantage in the continuing reform and privatisation of the public services.

In other words, if the people prefer to preserve values of collective responsibility, this may have an impact on governments. But 'the

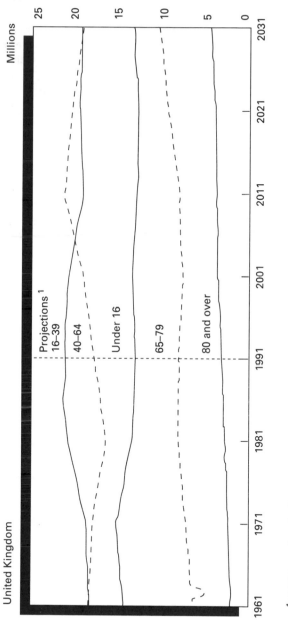

Figure 9.1 Population by selected age bands (*Source:* Central Statistical Office, *Social Trends 22,* London: HMSO, 1992)

people' do not all have the same interests. Very rich people may successfully protect their wealth from taxation while people with no income may be willing to be 'collectivist'. Since the top rates of personal taxation throughout the world have been harmonised to a level well below 50 per cent, the attitudes to taxation and public services of the very rich are probably less important than those of the wage and salary earning population. The very rich will make sure that they do not have to pay any more for the welfare state and will not use the main state services.

The impact can be illustrated in the case of services for the elderly. The government's intention is to shift the pensions burden onto employers and employees, with the state pension as a residual safety net for those who have no occupational pension.

If this is achieved, a major element of spending, social security and care of the elderly population, will in effect be shifted out of the state sector. In that case, for all those with private arrangements, including private health insurance, the defence of public provision and public services will increasingly be a matter of altruism rather than of self-interest. We saw in Chapter 1 that one reason for the difficulty in reforming the NHS was that the chief beneficiaries of the health

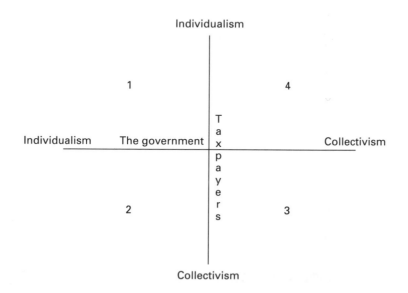

Figure 9.2 Collectivism versus individualism

service are the middle classes who support the Conservative Party. If that link is broken, and the middle classes are no longer dependent on, and therefore committed to, the welfare state, a large number of the influential voters will be more 'individualist' than 'collectivist'. It is worth considering a variety of scenarios in which 'the people', defined as income earners and taxpayers, and the government have predominantly individualist or collectivist values. In Figure 9.2 there is a matrix of possible combinations.

FOUR SCENARIOS

Scenario 1: the residualisation of the welfare state

In quadrant 1, the taxpayers and the government are all committed to individualism. This option means: 'if you can pay, you get it; and if you can't, you don't.' That is, services would be provided according to the customers' willingness and ability to pay. While this allows choice for the users, the amount of choice is constrained by the amount of money. This is already the case in the state school sector where people are making 'voluntary' contributions to keep the service intact. It is normally much easier to raise funds in those schools where the parents' incomes are high. Increasing private health insurance will ensure a two- (or more) tier system of healthcare, with a very basic level of state provision. Even in the area of public protection, where there is increasing use of private security companies, there would be differential access to protection. In effect, public services would become a residual, basic level of service for those unwilling or unable to pay.

In this scenario there is fragmentation with different 'markets' for different segments. For those relatively well-off people who are able and willing to contribute funds to services, there will be a high level of service. For the rest there will be reduced funds, tight budgets and a minimalist attitude to service provision and investment.

What does this mean for managers? In the affluent sector the emphasis will be on service quality, customer care and competitive behaviour to attract customers. In other words, there will be an outward-looking approach which emphasises the same issues with which competitive service businesses are concerned.

For the rest, the residual, the emphasis is on the management and control of expectations. 'Demarketing', or the suppression of demand for services, is more important than customer care which would only attract more users and therefore would be likely to break budget limits. Fund-raising may be an important part of the task of managers as state funding is restricted. However, the users are unlikely to be the best source of funds, and other efforts will be required.

For other aspects of public sector work, which are not about service provision, but rather about regulation and control, there will simply be less to do. Functions such as town and country planning, building control and environmental health control become less interventionist as they are seen as infringements of individual liberty and the spirit of enterprise.

Scenario 2: privatisation and charitisation of services

If the government follows an individualist line while the people are collectivist, this also implies the marginalisation of the state, but relies on a much greater use of charities and voluntary work. At the moment charities in the United Kingdom account for a very small proportion of the caring services. Even the large national charities have budgets which are tiny compared with those of local authorities: for example, the Spastics Society, which provides educational, residential and caring services for people with cerebral palsy, has an annual budget of £50 million, or the same as a single county social services department.

With a decreasing emphasis on state provision, but a willingness among the public and the voluntary agencies to take on more of the work of the welfare state, there will be new tasks. More managers will transfer from the traditional public sector to the growing charities. Those remaining in the public sector will have to spend more time encouraging the development and growth of the voluntary sector. The voluntary sector will try to maintain its identity and try to avoid becoming simply substitutes for and agents of the public sector. Managers in the public sector will try to achieve the opposite, developing more formal contracts with other agencies. This approach is close to Nicholas Ridley's 'enabling local authority' (see Brooke, 1989).

Planning of services will become much more haphazard: instead of planning the use of reasonably predictable resources, the provision of services will be dependent both on the existence of other agencies, which are unevenly distributed, and their ability to raise funds.

Implementation of the community care reforms implies that there will be sufficient private and voluntary agencies to take care of all the vulnerable people for whom the state accepts responsibility. This is unlikely to be the case unless the local authorities and health authorities promote the development of such organisations.

Scenario 3: the retention of the welfare state

Here, a future government responds to those opinion polls which suggest continuing support for public services. It also might decide that the rhetoric of cutting the public sector is counter-productive and, in future, level funding will be both the rhetoric and the reality. It could be that a Labour or coalition government is elected on a platform of preserving public services. Even here there is unlikely to be a complete reversal of many of the managerial changes that have taken place. For example, it is difficult to imagine any government repurchasing large numbers of ex-council houses from their new owner occupiers.

The 'welfare state' would be preserved, in that there would be universal access, equitably supplied, to a whole range of education, health and social services. It does not imply that all 'caring' is done by the state: still a very high proportion of sick, mentally handicapped and old people will be cared for within the family.

What are the implications for managers? Initially, it gives some relief from the constant search for both cost savings and self-justification. But in all services, there needs to be constant attention to providing services which gain support from the users and taxpayers. One of the reasons for the successful dismantling of the bulk of the public housing service was that for many tenants the service left the housing bureaucracies with an unacceptable degree of control over people's lives.

Scenario 4: the persuasive welfare state

The effect of having a collectivist state but an individualist controlling group in society is that people need to be persuaded that the services are worthwhile. There are important implications for the management of the welfare state. If the population of taxpayers and users of services is driven by individualism and consumerism, the services need to be provided in a way which meets those preferences. The emphasis should be on a 'customer orientation' to maintain support. This will be increasingly true as competition increases. If patients can choose their hospital, then the customer care aspects of hospital management, which is one way in which patients will judge the hospitals, will be given increasing attention. The response to individualism may be superficial, with better treatment by receptionists and telephonists, more respect for individuals' time in making appointments, a more individually responsive school curriculum in 'fringe' subjects.

Some local authorities lost public support during the 1980s. Poor services were further eroded by restrictions on spending. In some cases the response was to improve accessibility by opening area offices and other local access points. In other cases public relations and presentational improvements were made. These approaches only generate support if accompanied by genuine service improvements.

MANAGERIAL VALUES

Underpinning many of the recent reforms is a particular view of what 'management' is, and especially how the management of the public sector could be improved. Many of the recent reforms have been introduced by people from the private sector, either hired as temporary advisers, quite often accountants seconded from the big accountancy firms or, in some cases, imported permanently. For example, the procurement function for the armed forces was taken over by Peter Levene, a complete outsider to the civil service. We have already seen some of the missions in which Roy Griffiths has been involved, redesigning the management of the NHS and personal social services. This use of people from the private sector is partly based on a belief that the private sector has the best people. There is also a notion that the nature of management in the private sector is tougher, more exposed to competition and the chance of extinction and more 'bottom line'-oriented.

The managerialist ethic which has developed is based on the view that managers have 'the right to manage', which means that they should be in control of the organisations which they run and that they should be very proactive. Harold Geneen's book on management (1985) has a chapter called 'Managers must manage', by which he means:

> Managing means that once you set your business plan and budget for the year, you must achieve the sales, the market share, the earnings and whatever to which you committed yourself. If you don't achieve those results you're not a manager. . . . Things may be happening out there, for better or worse, but you are not making them happen. You're not managing them. It's not that you're mediocre or a bad manager. You're not a manager. (p. 83)

It is this view of managers as controllers which underlies many of the managerial reforms in the public sector. Administering systems which are in a steady state, and doing so by arriving at a consensus among managers of various departments and with the trade unions is not considered to be real 'management'. Real managers impose their will on their subordinates and on the trade unions.

Part of the managerial ideology is that there is no difference between running a factory and running a hospital, or between a company and a health authority. If there are differences, such as the fact that there is no market or there is no way of measuring profits, then these differences should be removed. If the hospitals are profit centres, or the schools run like businesses, then management can be similar to running parts of companies.

The managerial idea includes the notion that 'professional managers' with some academic qualification in management are the right people to run everything, including the public services. Qualifications such as a Masters in Business Administration would then be an appropriate general management background for running any organisation, whether in the public or the private sectors. It follows that any political accountability for the running of those services is inappropriate. Politicians would simply be interfering with the managers' rights to manage. Hence, for example, local authority representatives are removed from health authorities and school governors are recruited from 'business' because that automatically brings with it a managerial approach.

This view of management has also permeated large parts of the public sector which are still run by 'traditional' public sector managers. It is in conflict with some of the other values which permeate, especially in the professions. Headteachers have been heard to say, 'I did not come into teaching to be a manager and an accountant' when they are asked to run their school budgets.

Doctors say that they want to be free from budgetary and management constraints when choosing treatments for their patients. These people are expressing a form of professionalism which has three main features. First, the practitioners are autonomous from managerial structures which might be imposed from outside the profession. Second, standards are set by the profession itself and not subject to outside review. Finally, the 'customers' know less about what they need than the providers do. Naturally, when this sort of professionalism encounters the managerialist approach there are tensions, often between the desire to provide as good a service as possible and the desire to save money. These are often combined with a tension between being inward-looking, concentrating on procedures and systems, and outward-looking, listening to users and following their preferences. The narrow view of management can make organisations inward-looking, as can some aspects of professionalism.

If we put these two tensions together in public sector organisations we can see a conflict within the two sets of values (see Figure 9.3). Quadrant 1, where managers dominate and the main culture is inward-looking, produces an organisation obsessed with budgets and

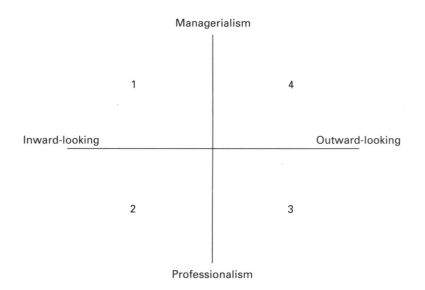

Figure 9.3 Managerialism, professionalism and orientation

procedures and forgetting about the users. Hence, for example, those local authorities which have gone through major reorganisations in the name of efficiency lose sight of their purpose and spend all their time meeting with each other, rather than finding better ways of serving the users.[3] Chief executives of such organisations spend all their time talking to other managers about their performance against targets, or simply on procedural matters, rather than making the organisation look towards its users. In quadrant 2, the professionals have taken over, but they are still inward-looking. Schools whose teachers are in control of the curriculum and teach according to their own standards rather than taking account of the abilities of the pupils or the needs of the communities of which they are part fall in this category. Schemes such as 'compacts' which try to guarantee jobs for school leavers from deprived backgrounds are designed to make the schools more outward-looking, while staying under professional control (quadrant 3).

Quadrant 4, in which the organisation is controlled by managers but is outward-looking, is the ideal implied by the managerialist ethic. It is assumed that competitive businesses constantly look outwards towards their customers. Management's job is to make sure that this happens. It is assumed that this is where current reforms will lead the public sector. But is this likely?

There is one crucial difference between businesses and the non-traded public sector. If businesses are outward-looking and customer-oriented, they generate sales which produce revenue. We saw in Chapter 7 that it is possible to make public services more user-oriented through careful service design. But what if that effort produces greater expectations and more demand for the services? A rationing process has to take place, unless there is an open-ended budget. Competition between individual units may create extra revenues for those units which are successful, but the total budget is still fixed. Once there is rationing combined with public accountability, there is a need for judgement. Professional and political judgements about who is entitled to what and who can benefit from what are quite different from judgements about what will sell.

This crucial difference, the fact that there is no 'sale' connecting the organisation to its users in the way companies are connected to their customers, means that the wholesale importation of private sector management techniques and the ideologies that go with them is inappropriate. There has to be a public sector management set of ethics which are appropriate to the management of the welfare state. This set will not necessarily be the same as those which were dominant when the institutions were established, nor those which have become dominant as those institutions have matured. What would they be?

PUBLIC SECTOR MANAGEMENT ETHICS

The right sort of exchange

If the management of businesses is built around the sale, the management of public services could also be built around the analogous relationship between the organisation and its users. We saw in Chapter 7 that there is a great variety in the relationship, from the user as customer to the user as prisoner. The crucial thing is to make sure that the service is appropriate to the relationship. Recipients of benefits should not be made to feel like criminals. Tenants should not be made to feel that they have no rights. This is not easy since there are inevitably different views about the relationship in different parts of the organisation. For example, the courts may have a different view of an appropriate relationship for convicted criminals from the probation service, or front line staff in hospitals may have a different view of the nurse/patient relationship from the management board of the Department of Health.

Service providers may have different views from users about what is the actual relationship. Some headteachers think that education is a privilege, while many pupils feel it is an imposition. Residents in old people's homes may feel like customers, while the staff treat them as beneficiaries of welfare.

Once the relationship has been defined satisfactorily and agreed with the users the whole of the management effort should be directed to supporting it with resources, with training, with encouragement. This is not always the case and management often seems to be directed towards spoiling the relationship.

Respect for the task: respect for the producers

An important aspect of the service relationship is the way the organisation treats its own workforce. If the organisation denigrates the task and devalues the workforce, then the service cannot be satisfactory. A demoralised workforce is unlikely to do more than a barely adequate job. In recent years there has been a progressive demoralisation of the workforce, especially the professional workforce, in many parts of public service. Relative pay, compared with the private sector, has declined, and in many occupations such as teaching, nursing and other medical professions the impact of 'efficiency savings' and budgets restraint has been a growth in stress and disillusionment. This is a sustainable management strategy only if certain other conditions apply. There must be a fast turnover of staff, so that people are able to leave and be replaced before their disillusion translates itself into the service relationship. Tasks must be defined and programmed in such a way that the fast turnover does not reflect itself in inconsistent service. Fast food outlets are like this. The workforce is generally poorly paid, there is a constant supply of untrained unskilled young people willing to take the jobs on a short-term basis, and the work is routinised so that minimal training is required. These conditions do not generally apply where the service is provided by people who require a long period of training and where the tasks require a degree of initiative and judgement. The education and health services are not McDonalds. In competing for employees, one competitive edge that the public sector can sustain is the chance of a worthwhile respected job.

Part of the respect for the workforce is a respect for their motivations. If the people in the organisation are working there to maximise their earnings, then the way in which the motivation scheme is devised should take that into account. However, if there is an element of 'public service' or some positive aspect of professionalism, that, too, should be respected. To introduce performance-related pay as though people's motivation to perform well was only determined by money will produce a demotivated workforce if they have other ideas. There is still a fund of goodwill among large parts of the public sector workforce which should be harnessed rather than dissipated.

Entitlement

Customers have rights and can choose how and where to spend their money and have a certain amount of legal protection against dishonest producers. When they make transactions they are clear about what they can expect from the seller.

In public service this relationship is often less clear. What precisely is a pupil entitled to expect from a school? Or a patient from a doctor? What is a candidate for a driving test entitled to expect from the examiner? And what services can any citizen reasonably expect to get from the institutions of the state? In many cases the exchange is loaded in favour of the producer. The balance can be redressed by establishing definitions of entitlements. In Canada citizens have legally enforceable entitlements from state institutions, including the education service. There have been some experiments with this in the United Kingdom.

The establishment of a clear set of expectations is of as much benefit to the organisation as to the users. If the staff are all clear about what the user expects, their job is easier to do. In too many cases the entitlement is not clear or it is handed down from the welfare state to the users. To be effective, entitlement must result from demands made actively. The consumer rights in the Citizen's Charter were never negotiated or even discussed with service users: they were made up by the people managing the services.

Service providers cannot be automated

All institutionalised services are a substitute for genuinely mutually beneficial exchanges. All the smiling and saying 'have a nice day' that goes on in the hotel and catering businesses (which are known internally as the hospitality industry) are really substitutes for the genuinely mutual hello-ing that goes on among friends and acquaintances. The difference is that the customers are paying for the hellos.

The same is true of the other aspects of an institutional service relationship which are defined either explicitly or implicitly by the fact that the user is paying the provider for it. This is unlike those relationships which provide the same sort of care outside a paying relationship, such as that between parents and children.

Establishing contracts for public services implies that this process could go a lot further. But should it? If it is the case that service providers are motivated by a desire to provide a good service, is specifying the service in such a way that it can be bought and sold (the commodification of the service) desirable?

The specification and contract are only desirable as sources of accountability. If there are no contracts, accountability exists only through the trust of the users and payers in the providers of the services. If the users trust the doctors to do their best and not to steal money, then we need only the flimsiest accounts of their spending and their actions. If we do not trust them, we wish to see detailed plans of what they intend to do and a detailed account of what they did and what they achieved. Very detailed specifications, such as those which fast food chains impose on their workforce, turn service providers into parts in a machine because the employers think that this is the only way to provide a good service.

Accountability

In the public sector the accountability structures make managers' jobs different from those of managers of private services. For example, a district health authority manager may be instructed to do all she or he can to keep a hospital open. The regional health authority may have different ideas and wish the hospital to close, as might the minister. Such ambiguous accountability has no parallel in the private sector, where managers are ultimately accountable to shareholders.[4]

Because of this ambiguity, an important part of managerial work in the public sector involves managing the relationship between the organisation and the political process. Simple models, in which the paid managers have a very clearly defined role which consists of implementing policy, rarely work out in practice. First, the services are in many cases run by managers who are also professionals, who have a legitimacy which arises from their professional status as much as their organisational position. Second, policies are often introduced onto the political agenda by managers, officials or professionals. Meanwhile, politicians like to get involved in management, whether a Minister of Defence who feels the need to have detailed involvement in the procedure for defence equipment procurement or a local councillor who feels that the nature of the management process in a local authority is an important part of politics.

Managerial work in public services therefore involves an important and complicated interface with the political process. The previously accepted ethic that managers do not work to further the interests of a particular party has been eroded. Managers need to be very clear about their degree of independence and the boundary between politics and management. If their work is too closely identified with a particular party, they may have to accept that a change of political power may bring a change of job.

User power

Accountability to the users of public services is also different from accountability of companies to their customers, which is exercised only through the buying and selling relationship. In the public services, the users cannot exercise their power through the exchange, often being powerless in the face of the institution whose services they are using. Paradoxically, because people do not normally give away power, the organisations have to transfer power to the users to make this relationship more equal. The principle should be: 'the users should be in control unless there are compelling reasons why they should not.' Unfortunately, this also involves individual managers giving up personal power, which they are reluctant to do.

Freedom and equality

In Part One we saw that the attitude of the reforming governments has been that freedom only comes from choice and individualism in the marketplace. Any restriction of individual choice, including the payment of taxes, is a step on the road to serfdom, according to Hayek and his supporters.

By definition, services are about collective choices and therefore restrict individual choices. If you pay tax to fund the health service, that restricts your freedom to spend that money on something else. You may pay willingly because you have a particular view about the value of collective healthcare, or you may be unwilling to pay the tax, although forced to do so. Either way you have no choice.

Although public services are firmly in the collectivist mould, there are still decisions to be taken about the way in which both individual and collective choices are made. The centrally planned and centrally controlled model, with no consumer choice, is one whose time has passed. But collective provision need not imply the erosion of individual choice.[5] Collective choices should be genuinely collective and not the result of a bureaucrat exercising power over people. If choices are to be made collectively, they have to be done through a democratic process. Where possible, services should also leave scope for individual choices.

The substitution of bureaucracy under indirect democratic control, either at national or local level was the post-war model for the welfare state. For the twenty-first century the welfare state needs to be in tune with the dominant values and to operate in an acceptable style. To achieve this, a new consensus has to be established between earners and the dependent population, and a new agreement between service users and service providers.

BUYERS AND SELLERS IN THE NEW PUBLIC SECTOR MARKETS

The fragmentation of the institutions of the welfare state and the division between buyers and sellers make managers think about their values. Sellers, or providers, have to run the organisation at least partly in a commercial way. This can make a difference to the way they choose whom to provide the services for, what prices to charge, how they treat the staff. The commercial accountability can remove their social obligations which now rest with the purchasers. The problem for the purchasers is how to meet their public obligations through contracts with providers. Purchasers themselves may be forced to contradict their public service values, for example if they are forced to purchase at the lowest price whatever their views of quality. In the area of community care, for example, quality can be affected significantly by small differences in price.

CONCLUSION

The public sector is at a confusing moment in its history. While the advocates of free markets claim that major reforms are still necessary, the users of public services seem to remain reasonably satisfied with them. Throughout the public services people feel that resources are scarce, although overall expenditure has remained fairly steady over recent years. The physical evidence supports the view that budgets are stretched. The state of the hospitals, schools, streets, social security offices and other public buildings does not suggest a well-funded, self-confident, proud public service. The contrast with other countries in Europe is striking, and even such bastions of the free market as Singapore and Hong Kong have public services which, on the surface at least, put the United Kingdom to shame.

What is to be done if there are to be well-run, adequately funded services which reflect the preferences and aspirations of the users? This book has indicated some answers. First, the level of funding for both public services in general and each service in turn should be based on the volume and quality of service and not on abstract ideas about reducing the percentage of GDP, or about a percentage change from the previous year's budget. The public expenditure process is currently an exercise in bargaining over shares of the cake over which the Treasury is the custodian. Obviously, limits have to be set, but the dialogue should include some definition of service standards throughout the public services.

Second, the services must be defined and designed in detail with their users. The idea that professionals and managers always know best applies only in very limited areas. One reason for the growing popularity of market ideas is that in a market exchange the buyer has a certain amount of power over the seller. Public services must find an equivalent way of empowering its users. This does not mean that all dealings should be financial transactions.[6]

Third, accountability can only be achieved if the services can demonstrate their achievements and results as well as their prudent use of resources. Performance measurement must be transformed into a positive device for communicating with service users and for demonstrating and celebrating success as well as for exposing and correcting shortcomings. If competition is an effective way of improving performance without detriment to the service providers, then it should be given a chance. If competition is only a device for reducing the pay and conditions of people who provide services, it will not bring about a sustained improvement in services because it devalues them. The front line staff are the key to the renewal of public services. If they do not get satisfaction and self-respect from their work, they will not generate satisfaction in the service users. If public services are to continue to be oriented towards their users, they will have to turn themselves upside down to concentrate on supporting the service/user relationship. Many aspects of the recent reforms present the possibility of doing this, although the old hierarchies will try to recreate themselves.

This may all sound Utopian. After all, the Thatcher decade is supposed to have produced an ethos of self-reliance and self-interest in which there is no room for public service. Perhaps; but it has not eliminated the need for income support, education, healthcare, public transport and the rest of the services which make a civilised society. Perhaps we shall be able to learn from the new Clinton government in the United States. Governor Clinton endorsed the book by Osborne and Gaebler (1992) who have shown that there are ways of managing public services which do not rely simply on privatisation and competition. Perhaps the United States may be turning away from Republican ideas about the public sector, many of which were similar to those of the British conservatives. Osborne and Gaebler's book is now being widely read in British government circles.

Many of the approaches we have suggested try to introduce responsive services in which the service users have choice and influence if not control over their services. If the economy is to recover and grow, the efficiency and quality of public services are vital elements in that recovery.

NOTES

1. Autumn Statement, November 1992, para. 2.10.
2. For a discussion on likely spending levels, see Glennerster (1992, ch. 15).
3. Even during decentralisations, managers' time is spent in establishing systems rather than in making the services more responsive.
4. For more detail on the different forms of accountability in the public sector, see Day and Klein (1987).
5. For a philosophical discussion of these propositions, see Norman (1987).
6. Le Grand and Estrin (1989) suggest that because purchasers are powerful, the only way to empower service users is to make them purchasers. All relationships between service providers and service users should involve buying and selling.

REFERENCES

Adam Smith Institute (1984), *The Omega Report: Health*, London: Adam Smith Institute.

Atkinson, A. B. (1989), *Poverty and Social Security*, Hemel Hempstead: Harvester Wheatsheaf.

Audit Commission (1986), *Making a Reality of Community Care*, London: HMSO.

Audit Commission (1988a), *Administrative Support for Operational Police Officers*, London: HMSO.

Audit Commission (1988b), *Delegation of Management Authority to Schools*, Occasional Paper 5, London: HMSO.

Audit Commission (1989), *Housing the Homeless: The local authority role*, London: HMSO.

Audit Commission (1992), *Developing Local Authority Housing Strategies*, London: HMSO.

Bacon, R. and Eltis, W. (1976), *Britain's Economic Problem: Too few producers*, London: Macmillan.

Bailey, R. and Trinder, C. (1989), *Under Attack? Public Service Pay Over Two Decades*, London: Public Finance Foundation.

Bains, M. A. (Chairman) (1972), *The New Local Authorities: Management and structure*, Working Group on Local Authority Management Structures, London: HMSO.

Barclay Report (1982), *Social Workers: Their role and tasks*, London: Bedford Square Press.

Beaumont, P. B. (1992), *Public Sector Industrial Relations*, London: Routledge.

Brittan, S. (1973), *Capitalism and the Permissive Society*, London: Macmillan.

Brittan, S. (1988), *A Restatement of Economic Liberalism*, London: Macmillan.

Brooke, R. (1989), *Managing the Enabling Authority*, London: Longman.

Burns, D. (1992), *Poll Tax Rebellion*, Stirling: AK Press.
Cabinet Office (1988), *The Next Steps*, London: HMSO.
Caldwell, B. J. and Spinks, J. M. (1988), *The Self-Managing School*, London: The Falmer Press.
Central Statistical Office (1992) *Social Trends 22*, London: HMSO.
Chadwick, E. (1859), 'Results of different principles of legislation and administration in Europe: of competition for the field as compared with competition within the field of service', Royal Statistical Society, 22, 381.
Chapman, L. (1978), *Your Disobedient Servant*, London: Chatto and Windus.
Coase, R. H. (1937), 'The nature of the firm', *Economica* NS, 4, 386–405.
Common, R. and Flynn, N. (1992), *Contracting for Care*, York: Rowntree Foundation.
Common, R., Flynn, N. and Mellon, E. O. (1992), *Managing Public Services: competition and decentralisation*, Oxford: Butterworth-Heinemann.
Conservative Party (1987), *The Next Moves Forward*, London: Conservative Party Central Office.
CPAG (1988), *Poverty: The facts*, London: Child Poverty Action Group.
Crain, W. M. and Ekelund, R. B. (1976), 'Chadwick and Demsetz on competition and regulation', *The Journal of Law and Economics*, XIX (Part 1), 149–62.
Cumes, J. W. C. (1988), *A Bunch of Amateurs: The tragedy of government and administration in Australia*, Melbourne: Macmillan.
Day, P. and Klein, R. (1987), *Accountabilities: Five public services*, London: Tavistock.
Deakin, N. (1987), *The Politics of Welfare*, London: Methuen.
Demsetz, H. (1968), 'The cost of transacting', *Quarterly Journal of Economics*, 82, 33–53.
DHSS (1980), *Inequalities in Health* (the 'Black Report'), London: HMSO.
Domberger, S., Meadowcroft, S. A. and Thompson, D. J. (1986), 'Competitive tendering and efficiency', *Fiscal Studies*, 7 (11).
Drucker, P. (1955), *Principles of Management*, London: Heinemann.
Durham, P. (ed.) (1987), *Output and Performance Measurement in Central Government: Some practical achievements*, Treasury Working Paper No. 45, January 1987.
Efficiency Unit (1988), *Management in Government: The next steps*, London: HMSO.
Flynn, N. (1988), *Decentralised Management in Social Services*, Project Report No. 4, Social Services Inspectorate, DHSS.
Flynn, N. and Walsh, K. (1982), *Managing Direct Labour Organisations*, Birmingham: INLOGOV.
Flynn, N., Leach, S. and Vielba, C. (1985), *Abolition or Reform?*, London: Allen and Unwin.
Freebairn, J., Porter, M. and Walsh, C. (eds) (1987), *Spending and Taxing: Australian reform options*, Sydney: Allen and Unwin.

Fulton, Lord John (1968), *The Civil Service*, Report of Committee, Cmnd 3638, London: HMSO.

Gamble, A. (1988), *The Free Economy and the Strong State: The politics of Thatcherism*, London: Macmillan.

Geneen, H. (with Moscow, A.) (1985), *Managing*, London: Granada.

Glennerster, H. (1992), *Paying for Welfare*, Hemel Hempstead: Harvester Wheatsheaf.

Goodin, R. E. and LeGrand, J. (1987), *Not Only the Poor: The middle classes and the welfare state*, London: Allen and Unwin.

Gretton, J., Harrison, A. and Beeton, D. (1987), 'How far have the frontiers of the State been rolled back between 1979 and 1987?', *Public Money*, 7 (3).

Griffith, B., Iliffe, S. and Rayner, G. (1987), *Banking on Sickness: Commercial medicine in Britain and the USA*, London: Lawrence and Wishart.

Griffiths, R. (1988), *Community Care*, London: HMSO.

Hampden-Turner, C. (1990), *Corporate Culture: from Vicious to Virtuous Circles*, London: Hutchinson.

Harris, R. and Seldon, A. (1979), *Over-ruled on Welfare*, London: Institute of Economic Affairs.

HMSO (1989a), *Working for Patients*, Cm 555, London: HMSO.

HMSO (1989b), *Caring for People: community care in the next decade and beyond*, Cm 849, London: HMSO.

HMSO (1991a), *The Citizen's Charter: raising the standard*, Cm 1599.

HMSO (1991b), *Competing for Quality*, Cm 1730.

HMSO (1992), *Choice and Diversity: A new framework for schools*, Cm 2021.

HM Treasury (1987), *Investment Appraisal in the Public Sector*, London: HMSO.

HM Treasury (1992), Autumn Statement, Cm 2096.

Hoover, K. and Plant, R. (1989), *Conservative Capitalism in Britain and the United States*, London: Routledge.

Hunt, J. (1986), *Managing People at Work*, 2nd edn, London: McGraw-Hill.

Jackson, P. (1982), *The Political Economy of Bureaucracy*, Oxford: Philip Allan.

Jesson, D., Gray, J., Ranson, S. and Jones, B. (1985), 'Some determinants of variations in expenditure on secondary education', *Policy and Politics*, 13, (4), 359–91.

Jesson, D., Mayston, D. and Smith, P. (1987), 'Performance assessment in the education sector: educational and economic perspectives', *Oxford Review of Education*, 13 (3), 249–66.

Jessop, B., Bonnett, K., Bromley, S. and Ling, T. (1988), *Thatcherism*, Cambridge: Polity Press.

Johnson, C. (1989), Introduction to 'The Market on Trial', *Lloyds Bank Annual Review*, 2, London: Pinter.

Johnson, N. (1990), *Reconstructing the Welfare State*, Hemel Hempstead, Harvester Wheatsheaf.

Judge, K. (1978), *Rationing Public Services*, London: Heinemann.

Keegan, W. (1984), *Mrs Thatcher's Economic Experiment*, London: Allen Lane.

King, D. (1987), *The New Right*, London: Macmillan.

Kogan, M. (1985), *Policy Making in Education*, Oxford: Oxford University Press.

Krieger, J. (1986), *Reagan, Thatcher and the Politics of Decline*, Cambridge: Polity Press.

Lawson, N. (1989), 'The state of the market', in Johnson, C. (ed.), 'The Market on Trial', *Lloyds Bank Annual Review*, 2, London: Pinter.

LeGrand, J. and Estrin, S. (1989), *Market Socialism*, Oxford: Oxford University Press.

LeGrand, J. and Robinson, R. (eds) (1984), *Privatisation and the Welfare State*, London: Allen and Unwin.

Likierman, A. (1988), *Public Expenditure*, Harmondsworth: Penguin.

Metcalfe, L. and Richards, S. (2nd edn 1990), *Improving Public Management*, London: Sage.

Mintzberg, H. (1983), *Structure in Fives: Designing effective organisations*, New Jersey: Prentice Hall.

Morgan, G. (1986), *Images of Organisation*, Beverly Hills: Sage.

National Consumer Council (1986), *Measuring Up. Consumer assessment of local authority services: a guideline study*, London: NCC.

National Consumer Council (1987), *Performance Measurement and the Consumer*, London: NCC.

National Institute for Social Work (1983), *The Barclay Report: Papers from a consultation day*, Paper No 15, London: NISW.

Normann, R. (1987), *Free and Equal: A philosophical examination of political values*, Oxford: Oxford University Press.

Normann, R. (1991), *Service Management: Strategy and leadership in service businesses*, Chichester: Wiley.

Nove, A. (1983), *The Economics of Feasible Socialism*, London: Allen and Unwin.

OECD (1985), *The Role of the Public Sector: Causes and consequences of the growth of government*, Economic Studies, No. 4, Spring 1985, Paris: OECD.

Office of Health Economics (1982), *Compendium of Health Statistics*, London: Office of Health Economics.

Osborne, D. and Gaebler, T. (1992), *Reinventing Government*, Reading, MA: Addison-Wesley.

Pascale, R. T. and Athos, A. G. (1982), *The Art of Japanese Management*, Harmondsworth: Penguin.

Pearce, D. W. and Nash, C. A. (1981), *The Social Appraisal of Projects*, London: Macmillan.

Peters, T. J. (1987), *Thriving on Chaos*, London: Macmillan.

206 *Public Sector Management*

Peters, T. J. and Waterman, R. H. (1982), *In Search of Excellence*, New York: Harper and Row.

Porter, M. E. (1980), *Competitive Strategy: Techniques for analysing industries and competitors*, New York: Free Press.

Public Finance Foundation (1991), *Swimming with or against International Tax Currents*, London: PFF.

Pym, F. (1984), *The Politics of Consent*, London: Sphere.

Quinn, R. E. (1988), *Beyond Rational Management*, San Francisco: Jossey-Bass.

Ranson, S. and Tomlinson, J. (1986), *The Changing Government of Education*, London: Allen and Unwin.

Riddell, P. (1983), *The Thatcher Government*, London: Martin Robertson.

Ridley, N. (1988), *The Local Right*, London: Centre for Policy Studies.

Rogaly, J. (1987), 'The Welfare State: tinkering rather than retailoring', in *The Thatcher Years*, Financial Times Publications.

Rose, R. (1989), *Charging for Public Services, Studies in Public Policy*, No. 172, Glasgow: Centre for the Study of Public Policy, University of Strathclyde.

Saltman, R. B. and von Otter, C. (1992), *Planned Markets and Public Competition*, Buckingham: Open University Press.

Savage, S. P. and Robins, L. (eds) (1990), *Public Policy under Thatcher*, Basingstoke: Macmillan.

Seldon, A. (1977), *Charge*, London: Temple Smith.

Slatter, S. (1984), *Corporate Recovery*, Harmondsworth: Penguin.

Society of Local Authority Chief Executives and Local Government Training Board (1988), *Managing Competition*, London: HMSO.

Stoker, G. (1988), *The Politics of Local Government*, Basingstoke: Macmillan.

Taylor-Gooby, P. (1985), *Public Opinion, Ideology and State Welfare*, London: Routledge and Kegan Paul.

Taylor-Gooby, P. (1991) 'Attachment to the welfare state', in R. Jowell *et al.*, *British Social Attitudes: 8th Report*, Aldershot: Dartmouth Press.

Toffler, A. (1987), *The Third Wave*, New York: Collins; London: Pan, 1987.

Townsend, P. (1987), in *The Financial Times*, 23 November.

Vickers, J. and Yarrow, G. (1985), *Privatisation and the Natural Monopolies*, London: Public Policy Centre.

Walker, A. (1984), 'The political economy of privatisation', in LeGrand, J. and Robinson, R. (eds), *Privatisation and the Welfare State*, London: Allen and Unwin.

Walsh, K. (1991), *The Impact of Competitive Tendering*, Department of Environment, London: HMSO.

Whitehead Report (1987), *The Health Divide: Inequalities in health in the 1980s*, Health Education Council. Now available in Townsend, P., Davidson, N. and Whitehead, M. (1988), *The Black Report*, London: Pelican.

Williamson, O. (1975), *Markets and Hierarchies*, New York: The Free Press.

INDEX

207

Index